# Preface

## What is included in a *Manual?*

A manual usually consists of the parts that make up the subject of the said *manual.*

It also includes a section on "troubleshooting" for when things are not working out as they should and you must evaluate the situation.

Then, there is a contact list of those available to assist you with the subject as a whole.

And finally, you'll find the warranty information and, in this case, there is no expiration of the subject.

Hopefully, there is also included a free, *lifetimes of service* adjustments with that warranty.

It also contains a method in which to contact the manufacturer.

# Acknowledgments

It might appear trite, thanking the same contributors to this book as the last two books. However, without their constant assistance and love, devotion and support there would never have been three books written by us, the authors.

Therefore, we want to thank those who love us unconditionally, first.

**I**sabella

**M**other *(& Harvey)*

**A**ngels *(Estes, Gabriel, Mariel, Raphael)*

**G**od

**E**lizabeth

To those who take their precious time to ask about us and our adventures in writing and/or read our first drafts, we thank you. Again, we will write your names in appreciation. Just as Estes records all of our names, yours are forever recorded in our manual.

*T.K., Paula, Heather, Becca, Diane and Gwen.*

1106 Design who edits, designs and configures our writings, we thank you for your total professionalism.

To Dave, "You've *carried* me, over six thousand years." Love, Carla

To Carla, "You are, and have been my strength and inspiration." Love, Dave

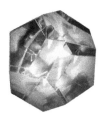

# Soul

The spiritual or nonmaterial essence of you that exists before and after the material/physical you that interfaces with the material/physical you and expresses itself as you, is defined as your *soul*. It is a divine spark from God, Tao, Source, Creator thus it is from and part of, but not the creator in whole.

All physical and nonphysical experiences of yours are recorded in the soul memory since your soul's creation.

Your experience right now, is in your present consciousness. All other past experiences exist in your subconsciousness. Who you are consists of all of your past experiences and all of your present experiences, right now!

The soul memory affects who you are at present. One example; frequently a birthmark in a current life can be correlated to a wound in a past life. How can this be possible? It's possible, only if the soul can influence the physical body and if the soul can affect *gene expression.*

*Gene expression* happens when the coded information in our DNA is converted into a physical trait, or body protein. It controls how we appear and how we function.

Why then, doesn't everyone have birthmarks, because certainly, everyone over thousands of years and reincarnations has had scars or wounds? The only conclusion must be that when the soul enters the body, it depends on the stage of the development of the fetus. Did the soul enter at conception, did the soul enter three months after conception or five minutes before the birth?

If the soul enters right at conception or shortly thereafter, gene expression will occur in the newly developing fetus. In this case, *both* biological gene expression and soul gene expression will develop the fetus. If the soul enters right before birth ... only biological gene expression will have affected the developed fetus.

Thus, if a soul entered early in the development, the fetus could develop a scar where a wound previously happened in a former life. However, if the soul entered just before birth, this fetus would not have developed a scar through soul gene expression. Because, this fetus would have only developed based on biological gene expression.

Therefore, this becomes much like the discussion of nurture versus nature or soul versus nature. Of course, both have an effect.

If scars can be developed this way, what other physical traits can be passed along through soul gene expression? It frequently is mentioned when looking at a photo of who you were in a past life, that there is something very familiar in the eyes and something similar in the appearance. Certainly, if you reincarnate along the same bloodlines you look very similar and this is frequently reported to be the case.

However, sometimes the reincarnation is not within close bloodlines yet there are very striking similarities. And at times, the photos look nothing like their previous incarnations. It would seem logical that a soul placed early in the developing fetus, through soul gene expression could alter the physical appearance more than the soul who is placed in the fetus just before birth.

So, we may look like our biological parents both physically and ethnically but we may also look like we did in a past life and still be somewhat affected both physically and ethnically by our parents.

As you will learn in the pages ahead, the soul waits to reincarnate and cycle back into reach the same tunnel that you have heard mentioned during near death experiences. As your time approaches, you will travel back through this same tunnel and enter the body of a developing fetus. This may occur at conception or any time during the pregnancy including just prior to birth. The way your soul affects your development is based on the time it enters the fetus and that is based on when the tunnel cycles and reaches you.

Therefore, the earlier your soul enters the fetus, the more it is affected by soul gene expression and the later it enters the fetus, the more the development is based on just biological gene expression.

The soul is a spark of the divine … God, Tao, Source, Creator. The soul is placed at a time, determined by the creator, in a manner that continues to affect your development. We will continue to explain how the creator places you and how that determines who you are and who you can become.

# Sacred Geometry

*Plato said, "God geometrizes continually."*

The dodecahedron has twelve sides, each with five borders. There are no parallel lines. Yet, the dodecahedron stacks upon itself with no void. Being stacked upon itself with no void causes every part to be connected. These twelve sides correspond to the twelve astrological signs, the twelve traits and the twelve archetypes of humanity.

Consider the helical design of DNA; a spiral turning in and upon itself not unlike a swirling matrix that appears as the symbol of infinity, all interconnected.

Just as DNA is made of four nitrogen bases which cause a structure in the physical, the four karmic issues of conceit, jealousy, selfishness and unforgiveness create a structure in the nonphysical. Two parents create the genetic foundation of our corporeal nature. The interaction between two souls creates the karmic foundation of our spiritual nature, drawing them together.

Now consider that all karma will eventually be replaced with love. The swirling matrix will contract and since there is no void, the matrix is filled with love. The love is then drawn to the love of God.

# Table of Contents

# Chapter 1
# Manuel – *Spanish meaning,* God is with Us

*Carla*

I love to use the expression, **"I never got the manual."** I am truly not trying to make excuses for myself or others. It would be better to admit, I just never knew how to travel through life. I used this term as a motivation because, I was always searching for the answers.

Dave and I were each raised God-fearing Catholics. That did not stop our overactive minds from wondering about life and how it all began … whether it could be explained with evolution theory, the Big Bang theory or creation by God. We were questioning everything we had learned and thought we knew up until this point in life, including what was real, what was invented and how we had come to exist. Neither of us had been very happy with ourselves or life. We needed some help.

One day, years ago we decided that meditation would benefit us in our daily lives and work. We were no different than every other human on Earth. We had stress and many questions about life.

Dave and I worked together in a medical office. I simply asked him one day, "Do you want to try meditation?" He agreed and that started our journey with meditation and the questions about life, death, God and just simply *why* about everything.

All those years of being a God-fearing Catholic did not mean I hadn't kept exploring. I had never believed that religion completely explained everything. I had spent years questioning it and reading and researching the truth and nontruth about religion. Over the years, I had attended several churches of varying denominations. My theory has always been that if God did not want me to think, I would not have the ability to question, therefore I continued to.

So, I wasn't surprised that my mother, who had passed away before I ever met Dave, had appeared to Dave while meditating on our third day of meditation.

On the next day of meditation, Dave was introduced to his Spirit Guide, Isabella. She has consistently appeared to him to this date, seemingly at his beck and call. She scolds him when necessary, advises him constantly like a best friend and appears immediately when he needs her. I love this being. She is dependable, which is a rarity. She is funny, nurturing, practical and all-loving. Shortly thereafter, we met Elizabeth, my Spirit Guide. She has been with me since my original birth, over 6,000 years ago. She is sweet, loving and always there where I can hear her in my left ear. Elizabeth is always present to remind us that, *love is a choice and an action.*

"You have many guides, but I will be with you forever," Isabella told Dave. "I've been with you since your original birth, six thousand years ago."

Isabella is always there for Dave. So is my mother. If my mother seems like she's not apparent, we ask for her, and she comes.

To create a visual that was easy for us to understand, I asked Dave to describe exactly what he saw in meditation. He drew pictures, and we started to keep a journal of what he was seeing and feeling. Besides the "seeing part" of the experience at that point,

Dave was feeling what Isabella and Mother were telling him, not hearing it. "It is hard to explain, but I don't hear them like we do when someone speaks to us out loud," he said.

He also has the ability to speak with passed-over souls but is discouraged in doing so.

Isabella explained that many passed-over souls, waiting to reincarnate carry negative karma which should not be experienced or interpreted. Some passed-over souls will try to influence the future once they find an open portal. They are trying to prepare the world that they are about to return to. Learning the future is never acceptable as it interferes with your individual choices and path.

Isabella explains Dave's gifts as clairaudient (hears in past lives and with spirit world), clairsentient (feels in past lives and feels in spirit world communication), clairvoyance (seeing past lives and the spirit world) and clairalience/clairgustance (smells/tastes while in past lives) in fact all five senses are present. Dave was unaware of his gifts up until this point. He always felt a spiritual connection with God but was very unaware of his other strengths. Having listed his above capabilities, Isabella clarified that no one has the ability of all knowing, which is claircognizance. Because, Dave is only privy to what is *shared* with him and only God is all knowing.

We began asking many questions. Some of our inquiries were in regard to where our Angels and Spirit Guides come from. We've heard them referred to as guardian angels, higher self, ascended masters, spirits, Mother Mary and passed-over loved ones. We just wanted to know the difference between all of them, who they were, what we call them, how we got them and what their purpose was in each of our lives.

We were asking ourselves and began asking Isabella all of the typical questions about life and its purpose. How did it all begin? And, what the heck were we doing here, living, existing or pursuing our purpose?

*Dave*

One night while meditating, Isabella shared with me the following. These are Isabella's words, verbatim:

From the beginning, there was always **One.** Complete in every way, God's male side was love, God's female side was inspiration. The love was like vital energy and the inspiration was like creation. One God in wholeness, completed by unity with male and female qualities. The joining of love and inspiration equaled one. That is God's wisdom. The wisdom is from completeness.

Then, an explosion started it all.

All of creation occurred.

Isabella continued to explain that God shared love with the Angels when they were created, never to be separated from God. They honor God's presence, are bathed in *love* and are in awe of God's presence. There is no choice. They cannot fathom God's absence, ever.

The infinite spread of God's reach is an ever-expanding universe and Heaven.

*Creation from nothing.*

*Light from nothing.*

*Then, there was darkness.*

*The heat was immense. Too hot for light.*

*Then the heat cooled. Thirteen billion years had passed.*

*The energy slowed and then again there was light from vibration. God matched the vibration and created all souls.*

From one-fourth of the vibration he created Spirit Guides. The vibration of the Spirit Guides matching the vibration of the souls.

Matter formed, then the pull of matter called gravity.

Then there were stars.

The earth was a speck in the solar system, the solar system a speck in the galaxy, the galaxy but a speck in the ever-expanding one and only universe, surrounded by God and Heaven.

The earth was unique, warm and cold, wet and dry and rotating about the sun. The oceans and the land formed.

There was combining of atoms, and then cells.

Evolution occurred in the sea, air and on the land.

The human was evolving, with the vibration in the human mind matching the vibration of the light.

The vibration could be present in Heaven and on Earth. This being could now understand choice, different from the animals.

God placed the first souls, over six thousand years ago, when the human was ready. The human was placed in stewardship of Earth.

God first placed a soul in woman and said, "You will be inspiration, creation, the Tree of Life, strength and beauty, both. You will bear the future."

God then placed a soul in man and said, "You will be her love, vitality, partner and equal; complete, only together." Together the two will possess wisdom, they do not have apart.

God's commandment was to *love* one another and choose the path back home to "I AM."

Thus, they will be the example for their offspring to *love* one another, create with one another, grow with one another and learn from one another, each one important, separately.

*God's commandment to love one another is meant for all forms of love.*

## So, what does God expect?

Human choices are not always wise, Isabella told us. Yet, like a loving parent, you are given life after life and chance after chance. God does not get angry, just disappointed. The lessons must be learned. You must learn what *love* is with acceptance of who you are and who others are. *Love* shared makes you whole. You must learn what *love* is not; not *conceited,* not *selfish,* not *jealous.* You must *forgive* those who act this way. They still have lessons to learn.

*Love* and inspiration, vitality and creation, human enlightenment or wisdom; meditation and prayer will help you.

Choose the correct path, which is **LOVE.** That is the struggle of the human soul. It may take many lives but you are never alone. We are here to help you. Our Spirit Guides are actually God reaching out to us. God's vibration is unique to us through our Spirit Guide. God's light matches the vibration to us. Thus, when our vibration had raised to a higher level, our soul was prepared for its first incarnation. The human soul does not fully appreciate that their vibration is one with God. Thus, the human soul attempts to elevate its own vibration. That soul, however, is not experienced enough to elevate its own vibration. Because, that soul concentrates on itself only.

What was God's plan for humankind? God created us with the intention for us to grow with both masculine and feminine qualities. And, by that, God meant that we need our qualities to encompass both masculine and feminine aspects such as empathy, gentleness, compassion, sensitivity, humility, stability, strength, courage, independence, assertiveness and cooperation. This was God's plan: Create a being who could grow, help one another to grow, *love* and share; even if it took more than one lifetime. Let me confirm. God used wisdom to create each of us with male and female qualities. Since we are each created uniquely, we each have different levels of those qualities but together we would be complete, partnering to grow. Our strengths would complement each other. Choosing a path back to God was the design from the beginning.

Just like any parents, in the beginning, God provided for our basic needs, as we were infants. We evolved from human-like creatures and when our souls were in vibration with God, and able to understand the consequences of our choices, God placed souls in the early women and men. We were above the animals but only through our mental abilities. ***We could all hear God, in the beginning.*** We were born to those with instincts just like other animals but without souls. We needed food, shelter and each other. All animals start this way, in need of protection and guidance. But God made us creatures with lessons to learn. That was the difference.

The instinct for self-preservation is basic to our survival. Without this, we and the animals would not flourish, but die off.

We grow through stages. It starts with the basic needs of food, survival and belonging, like an infant. We start to become aware of others. The human being then learns to compete to survive and belong.

It is our choices that must be nurtured. God gives us Spirit Guides and Angels for the very reason as to nurture us. When we are aware of others, we become aware of what they have. Do they have more than we have? Do we have more than them? Are they better than us? Are we better than them? These are questions that halt our growth. Killing another is possibly the greatest form of *conceit, jealousy* and *selfishness.* Placing ourselves before another, robbing them of their chance to learn and grow is stealing their chance to *love* and complete their path. This is the very nature of the human existence. That which is ***conceited, selfish, jealous*** and ***unforgiving*** lowers our vibration taking us further from God and the light and vibration.

Just like children, we must be taught to share and be happy with what we have and who we are. We are taught not to covet or want to be someone else or what they have. We are special just as we are, but not more special than another. ***Differences are our own uniqueness. Differences do not make us better, just different. We all have different gifts.***

Life after life we come back as someone different. We must learn the other side of the experience. Each time we return to Earth, a Spirit Guide and Angels assist us. We are never here alone.

Again, those actions which are *jealous, conceited, selfish* and *unforgiving* lower our vibration and take us further from the light which is God and those actions which arise from *love* raise our vibration and bring us closer to God or the light. In all reality, this is the definition of karma.

■ ■ ■

We have all lived many lives. Because, God has given us chance after chance like any other loving parent. One of our many lives is as the authors, Dave and Carla. Another life together, was as Giovanni and Katrina during Italy's renaissance period.

Each of our lives is filled with unique lessons in the attempt to overcome our karma. In each life, we are born under a different astrological sign again to grow and overcome; this comes in the form of help from God.

Katrina and Giovanni's story weaves throughout *The Manual* to guide us and to display to us just how marvelous God is at creating our experiences. God created us with freedom and free-will, guiding us with lesson after lesson and test after test and all the while providing us with assistance from our Astrological Sign, Trait, Archetype, Angel and Spirit Guide.

### Giovanni and Katrina ...

Katrina Rosetta Carlotta Farnese was born in Rome, Italy, in 1504 as a **Libra**. She was the illegitimate daughter of Cardinal Alessandro Farnese (the future Pope Paul III) and Mattea Orsini.

Katrina contracted polio as a child which caused her right leg to wither and, therefore, use a crutch to walk. She wore a long cloak to protect not only her leg but also her pride. She felt entitled due to her father's position and believed others were beneath her.

She also believed that others were judging her frailty as weakness when, in fact, she judged others on everything.

Ms. Orsini and Katrina traveled to the Apothecary every other week to purchase the necessary medication to treat her polio.

The Apothecary was owned by Armando Caponi and run by him and his son Giovanni. Giovanni came into the world under the sign of **Aquarius.** Giovanni, by the time he worked in his father's apothecary, had studied medicinal chemistry and Latin at Sapienza, the University of Rome.

The interactions between Katrina and Giovanni were anything but friendly during the many visits Katrina and Ms. Orsini made to the apothecary.

Giovanni attempted to make their communications sweeter by offering Katrina hard, cherry candy on her visits. Giovanni's sweet nature and gentleman-like manner impressed Katrina as well as her mother. The offering of the candy also somehow softened the arrogance of the **Aquarian** outer shell in Giovanni toward the haughty, condescending Libra, Katrina, difficult as it was.

Giovanni's habitually forced conversation with her by addressing her as, "Katrina," eventually took its toll. Katrina's sanctimonious response, "Giovanni!" was less than friendly and humble. However, one day in anger, Katrina spun around on her crutch, losing her balance and falling toward the ground. Giovanni ran to catch her, preventing her fall.

Giovanni's words surprised and stunned Katrina to the point of speechlessness. He said, "I will always catch you when you fall, Katrina."

Ms. Orsini was beginning to believe her daughter's rude and unfriendly behavior was more than conceit and perhaps was to cover her true feelings toward Giovanni. Thus, Ms. Orsini in an attempt to procure the relationship between her daughter and this wonderfully kind and "interested young man," whispered to Giovanni upon her leave, "Katrina is quite taken with you."

Ms. Orsini daily visited the local fruit-and-vegetable market where she would discuss her innermost thoughts with her friend and confidant, who happened to be the owner of the market.

*To be continued ...*

# IN GOD'S ...

**I**sabella,

**M**other

**A**ND

**G**od,

**E**lizabeth

Our lives, each individual one is uniquely created by God. We are not "cookie cutter" and each creation is ***personal!*** God gives a portion of God's self to each and every creation. In Hebrew, this is *Ahav* and *Ahava*, meaning to give in love and to give without expectation. Creation is literally in God's *IMAGE*. It is personal!

It is so personal that God gives another portion of God's self in the form of Angels and Spirit Guides to remind us, with freedom comes responsibility.

We can cocreate in the *IMAGE* of God or in any other way that we choose. However, if we choose to create in any other way than in the *IMAGE* of God, there are consequences. We are responsible for the consequences that are of our own creation. We are created in perfection at our first incarnation. It is in the choices we make during that first incarnation that change us from perfection to humans living with conceit, jealousy, selfishness and unforgiveness. When we are reincarnated that second time and thereafter, God carefully and specifically designs each of our personalities with **Astrological Signs, Traits** and **Archetypes.**

Consider how beautiful it truly is that we were designed with the potential to create ourselves in God's *IMAGE,* in the absence of conceit, jealousy, selfishness and unforgiveness.

The following pages are, indeed, personal messages from our Spirit Guides, from our family members who have passed over and from God.

*The Manual with Isabella, Mother and God, Elizabeth* is a glimpse into the personal plan God has created for each of us. Each one of us is unique and each life-design from God is individual and *personal* including each of our Atonements or Past-Life Reviews.

# Part I

## Isabella

## Chapter 2

# Isabella Speaks

*Isabella, derived from Hebrew word Elizabeth …*
*meaning, "God is my Oath."*

I am spark, light, eternal flame, together and completely separate. I am, as if, a ray of sunlight from God. I am not God but of God; the ray that connects you to God. I am not a tether. I am God's hands. When I reach out, it is God reaching out. I vibrate as you vibrate. When you vibrate higher, I vibrate higher. And, that vibration pulls you closer to God. I am closer to you than you can comprehend. And, you are closer to God than you will know until you return home.

I am both rainbow bridge and the light at the end of the tunnel. I am never separate from God and neither are you. The extension of God engulfs me … just as it engulfs you.

I am complete and yet incomplete. I fully understand and feel God's love. Yet, I fully feel you. When I feel your love, it is beautiful. When I do not, it pulls me away from God. At that moment, I feel the pull of God's love even greater if that is actually possible. It is as if God loves you more when you pull away.

*It is also as if I am one with God and one with you. The only thing that keeps me from being pulled apart is that God's love is complete and will not let me go.*

*As I am one with God, God will not let you go. You are God's choice. And, with that choice, comes love.*

*My sole purpose is to learn and understand your emotion. It is your ego and free will that separates you and my being from the love that created you. Yet, it is so simple. I was created because God will not let you go. If you truly choose to love, then there is no barrier to the pull that will bring you home.*

*I am but one ray, one spark, yet God is endless rays and endless sparks. I cannot fathom the love of God so strong that it continues to pull me to God. You cannot fathom how strong the love is that pulls of these endless rays and sparks and holds them to God.*

*Love, Isabella.   Please, thank you and you are welcome!*

*Isabella's version of the story before Kat and Gio ...*

In their previous lives, as Henry and Sussan, before they incarnated as Giovanni and Katrina, Giovanni had been brought into the world as a **Sagittarian** and Katrina was born under the sign of **Taurus.**

Henry had been born into his world under a role of leadership. As in many royal families, the role of leadership can be thrust upon you at a very young age and without your acceptance.

The **Sagittarian** tendency to believe you are all knowing and achieving, perhaps protected young Henry during this lifetime. Being thrown into power at such a young age, gave way to the arrogance of the **Sagittarian.** It actually assisted him in his life situation.

Katrina being Sussan, in her previous life, was born like many young women without control of her station or her future. She was born a pawn to the political process of power. This contributed to Katrina in her next life, wanting stature in that life. Being that she was born a **Taurus** as Sussan, added to her stubbornness and resilience to the life she was about to live.

When the life of Sussan became excessively abusive, Sussan was able to fight back due to her natural ability as a **Taurus** to succeed.

As Henry and Sussan matured, they relied on each other's strength to literally survive and their love grew. Life was exceedingly difficult as an unloved king and his hidden mistress with their child. Henry and Sussan required one another to survive. They needed the next lesson as well, which would come in the next life as Giovanni and Katrina.

Henry and Sussan needed each other to actually survive a difficult, hidden life without much meaning. Giovanni and Katrina needed each other to grow, not survive, which is why we incarnate on Earth again.

*To be continued ...*

# Part II

## Mother

# Chapter 3
# Mother and Harvey Speak

*Carla's mother passed away in 1996 from a brain tumor.*

*Mother* (Carla's mother)

*I never got the manual, either. Once I became a mother, I started to raise my five girls as good little Catholics. I tried to teach them what I knew about right and wrong; that included teaching them proper etiquette and the rules of life. From a very young age, I attempted to instill in them, "This is not how little girls act" when they misbehaved.*

*I stayed in a marriage much too long. I guess I was trying to teach my girls the meaning of commitment in the marriage and with their father. Commitment is an excellent lesson. However, commitment without self-respect was not the lesson that I should have been teaching them. The lesson should have been to respect yourself, try your best and treat others with the same respect you would like in return.*

*Amongst the lessons, there were many rules. Some of these were simply the rules I was taught by my own parents. Sometimes, I taught them rules without explanation. Many times, the* explanation became, "Because I said so!" I believed all little girls required boundaries and security from the outside world. Perhaps, I should have allowed my girls to ask the question, "Why?" a bit more often.

However, I was not always given the opportunity to ask, "Why?" myself, in my upbringing or in my marriages. I suppose we teach what we know and often what we know … hurts. In retrospect, I was trying to protect my daughters from the hurt.

I still believe we need rules. I hoped by following the rules my girls could survive life and avoid pain, as I hadn't. So, I can only hope I taught them enough about what to do and not do. Yet, somehow the "Why?" still matters. I wish I had encouraged them to ask more questions about life and rules. The problem still lies in the truth, that not everyone follows the rules.

I wish I had taught my five girls how to respond to the others who continue to not follow the rules. However, I had no clue myself.

I now know this answer lies somewhere between respect of others and respect for yourself. It includes equality, love, compassion, acceptance, forgiveness and non-judgement; for judgement belongs to God. The most important lesson I should have given to my five little girls was that a relationship where you are required to not be yourself is not a healthy relationship.

All the rules of life are about being our best selves … our unique self and not the self someone tells us to be. I guess I should explain, "Why." God created us unique and perfect as we are. And, as I learned myself, during my final life review, God said, "We need free will to love."

Love, Mother.   Thank you and please, out of respect, I will defer a portion of my discussion to another parent …

*Dave's father passed away in 2012 from*
*complications of Parkinson's Disease.*

*Harvey* (Dave's father)

*I ended the last twenty years of my career as a high school principal. I was the second to arrive at school every day; the janitor being the first to get there. Each and every day, my ritual was to prepare a pot of coffee for the teachers and carry two cups of the coffee to the boiler room.*

*I would sit in my suit and tie, drinking coffee and conversing with the janitor Emile, wearing his overalls. I instilled in Dave, "Not only should I respect the janitor, I should respect his wisdom." Many times, Emile knew more about the students than most of the teachers. He often knew, long before the teachers, the students who were struggling.*

*Emile would speak with a slight German accent, not unlike my own father's. I often wished the conversation with my father would have the same meaning as the conversations with Emile. Emile was so much more than a janitor in the school where I was the principal. He was a father, a husband, and my friend.*

*Emile had great love for his wife and son, yet, his love did not stop there. In some way, Emile loved every student that passed through those halls. Taking care of the school building was his way of giving something back to the rest of the world and the students in it.*

*The janitor would often say, "If I treat this building with respect, maybe the students will also." So, I thought ... what a wise man. Then, I told myself, "If I treat these students with respect, maybe they will learn to respect themselves."*

*One day, my friend Emile told me, "The other day, a kid dumped half of his lunch on the floor and walked out. So, I cleaned* up the floor. *All of the other students sat and watched me. The next day, that same student repeated his actions, dumping his lunch on the floor. Four boys on the other side of the lunch room got up. They picked up the lunch from the floor and placed it in the trash. The next day, as the same student finished his lunch, the same four boys walked over to him. They took his tray, and neatly dumped it in the trash can themselves. What Emile said after that story stuck with me. He said, "Harvey, find out what is wrong with that student."*

*Emile was not angry with the student for his disrespect but rather concerned with the feelings of the student who obviously was contending with something in his life. The other four boys were actually learning about respect but there was something in this boy crying out for help and attention. Emile was not just the janitor.*

*As a father and as a principal, it was my job to enforce the rules. We must all learn some sort of limits. There are consequences for our actions. This is the way the world works and this is the way God works.*

*All we can hope for is that our sons and daughters will learn lessons based on the rules and the wisdom that we share with them. Just as Emile shared his wisdom with me, I hope I shared my wisdom with my son. And, just as Emile's wisdom stated that the boy was acting out but not completely lost, he just simply reminded me to reach out, just as God would ... because none are lost.*

*Love, Harvey.*

*Mother's version of the story of Kat and Gio ...*

It's so interesting, the parallels. When I look at my past life now, compared to my past life then, they were not so different. I spent a great deal of time teaching etiquette. Very early on, I taught Katrina to set the table for a proper tea. We had owned a set of gold-rimmed tea cups. I taught her that she must treat the teacups with respect because of their value. We must take care of those things that have value.

Katrina broke one of the teacups as a small child and I expressed my anger. Here I was living a life of privilege, valuing things rather than my daughter. Certainly, the lesson to take care of your things is a good one. However, it implied to my **Libra** daughter, that things were of more value than her or people. Subliminally, this taught Katrina that a life of privilege was somehow important. This simply added to the tendency of **Libras** to be obsessed with material things.

What other things had I taught her? What began as an affair of passion with the Cardinal Farnese, became my acceptance of a life with privilege but no commitment. Where is the lesson about self-respect in those teachings?

Little did I know, my own actions were teaching Katrina much more than any etiquette lessons I could teach her. When I would hush my daughter about my lover/her father and his position, it taught Katrina that somehow I was flawed. This, in turn, taught her to see herself as flawed without perfection, with a withered leg from polio.

If I did not value myself more than that gold-rimmed teacup, how could I expect my daughter to read between the lines and value herself with imperfections.

Inadvertently, I had taught my daughter that our way of life was more important than the love that had created her.

I had loved her father but settled for no commitment. This was my choice. However, I should have taught my daughter that the choice always belonged to me/you. We do not have to settle for a part-time man.

If I acted as if appearance was more important than substance, it was not surprising that Katrina was so concerned with her withered leg and perfection.

So, I had taught Katrina to read, to paint and to love art. I also taught her to read poetry and to sing. However, I never taught her to dance. I thought if I involved her in those other things, she would never miss dancing. I taught Katrina how to communicate with other learned women. It would have been more of a life-lesson, to teach her to dance and overcome her insecurities.

Then, she may have learned the proper etiquette of talking with a gentleman and she may also have learned that it was alright to fall.

Katrina's need for medication continued until around the age of eighteen. Her doctor informed me that the polio medication would no longer affect the outcome of her disease. She would grow no more, the weakness in her leg would not improve nor would it be necessary to take the medication.

During our visits to the apothecary, I suspected that Katrina was actually finding joy in her interaction with Giovanni. I hesitated to end her joy. Giovanni appeared to have actual fondness for Katrina as well. What need would we now have for visiting the apothecary?

My daily visits to the local fruit-and-vegetable market had made my acquaintance with the owner of the market possible. His name was Horatio Albini. I grew to become accustomed to the wisdom of my new friend and confidant. Horatio was aware of the ongoing, developing relationship between my daughter and the son of the apothecary owner. He offered practical advice on a regular basis as he also was a father of three daughters.

I had shared with Horatio the doctor's opinion on Katrina's need for medication no longer. I also shared my despair in knowing Katrina would no longer have need to visit Giovanni and that there would be no further advancement in the healing of her polio. I feared she would become despondent and lose all hope for her future.

Horatio's words were as follows, "Poetry and art are more beautiful when shared. When Katrina realizes that she possesses something that can be shared, she will also realize she is more than merely a withered leg." He further went on to suggest Katrina and I continue to visit the apothecary and to find a reason to converse with Armando, leaving Katrina alone with Giovanni. Horatio, with pointing finger, advised that I not meddle in their business but reminded me that sometimes in youth we need help seeing what is front of us.

Horatio also reminded me that he was in the business of selling fruit and vegetables. He said, "I sell because the farmer plants the seed. My suggestion is to tell the boy, Katrina is quite taken with him, you know. And, let it go on from there."

*To be continued ...*

## Etiquette ... what is it?

What happened to walking on the right side of the hallway? All of us older than sixty years of age like to say, "Well, in the old days." So, since we fit that description, we'd like to say that in the old days, people walked to the right in halls, roads, sidewalks and so forth, because it gave some structure to the many persons all walking or driving in both directions. We now notice, walking through the mall, people walk everywhere and in every direction. Why? Is it defiance to do whatever we want? Is it lack of respect for others? Is it to just simply be different? Whatever the intention, it's not working. There is lack of organization, structure, politeness and respect everywhere in the world today.

We need to go back to the basics. Why can't we choose to walk on the right side? This is not to disrespect the *Lefty;* this is not to control anyone or buck someone else's culture. This is simply a means of creating less havoc. Creating less havoc reduces stress and conflict. Conflict makes everything a competition. In a competition, there is always a winner and a loser which makes everyone lose.

Love, which makes the world go round … is about cooperation and compassion not competition. Etiquette is about respect and cooperation. It is not about control or position. Holding the door for a woman is not because she's a meek, weak woman, it is simply respectful to hold the door for the person behind you … young, old, female, male etc.

It's just the right thing to do. Be kind, respectful and considerate. Do we really not have the time to do these things? Respect begets respect and kindness begets kindness. But someone has to start. Couldn't we all start it together? The action to not be respectful is the same as being disrespectful. And, this all begins with self-respect.

Why set the dining room table in a proper manner? And, with that, we mean with plates, and the knife on the right, fork on the left, glass above the knife, napkin next to the fork; just as if we were at a fancy restaurant dining out. The reason is quite simple. Because, in the big picture, it doesn't really matter where the utensils and plate sit. What matters is that we respect each other enough to organize our space and respect each other enough to organize our spaces together.

Why do we wait until the host or hostess is seated to begin our meal? Because, we respect their effort to prepare the meal. It's just kindness rather than selfishness. By all means, if the host or hostess says to start without them, then eat. But, even in restaurants today, this selfishness is reflected in the delivery of the meals. The servers will bring the meals out one at a time and promote eating ahead of one another. It's easier for them, which is selfish, but again, promotes lack of consideration. The meal, like any human interaction, is to be shared; the experience and the food. The opportunity for interaction should never be wasted. That is why we are here, after all. All forms of disrespect are forms of conceit; when you place yourself before another!

Etiquette is actually a way to avoid disrespect. Using your manners is always respectful.

And, etiquette is just the unofficial rules which help us avoid conflict.

Disrespect and using bad manners all stem from not taking responsibility for our own actions. Let's say we are in the public restroom and we throw the paper towel in the trash but it doesn't quite make it. Do we pick it up or do we walk away and leave it for someone else to throw away? Isn't that not taking responsibility for our own actions? It starts with those little things and compiles into the big things in life. I got fired but it couldn't have been my fault. I got divorced but it couldn't have been by any of my actions. I went to jail but it couldn't be because I wrote a bad check or didn't pay my parking fines. When do we choose to step up and just admit that we are not perfect? Do the right thing … use etiquette.

What happened to saying *PLEASE* and *THANK YOU*? Are we so conceited to believe that we are above being thankful? Respect goes in many ways. We should hold the door but we should also say, "*You are welcome*" when they say, "*Thank you!*" When we are shown respect, it should be acknowledged by us. These are simple acts toward the trickling down of respect and kindness that have gone wayward.

In many ways, this is about equality. Respect given is respect acknowledged. It should never be that *RESPECT* is *EXPECTED*. Without returned respect, it is simply conceit. Respect can only be given because it is an aspect of love.

Many are under the assumption that they earn respect and deserve it. However, love must be given freely. And, love must be equal and mutual. Therefore, respect should also be equal and mutual.

The opposite of respect is contempt and contempt is seated deeply in hate. Thus, disrespect is considering a person beneath you worthless and beyond consideration.

So, the next time someone is kind to you or holds the door for you, please say, *"Thank you."* Anything else is down right contemptable.

Therefore, when God says, "Treat others as you would expect to be treated yourself," it really means, "Remember your karma. If you just let the door slam on someone's face, can you expect God to leave the door open to Heaven for you?"

### More of Kat and Gio's story ...

So, on that day when Ms. Orsini had the perfect opportunity to suggest to Giovanni that perhaps her daughter was quite taken with him, Giovanni's response was, "Oh, it's hard to tell."

Their cat-and-mouse game continued for ten more visits where Giovanni would extort a greeting from Katrina, after having given her a piece of hard, cherry candy to sweeten her up!

Because of Giovanni's impeccable etiquette, he knew to discuss with Ms. Orsini the possibility of having an audience with her daughter. Ms. Orsini agreed and later informed her daughter of the date.

Their first date consisted of discussing art in their parlor with Ms. Orsini close by. They also enjoyed tea in their most precious ivory teacups with gold rims. While Ms. Orsini prepared the tea, Katrina took the opportunity to grill Giovanni about his aspirations for life and their future. Giovanni confessed that he was unsure that there would be a future for them together. Katrina admitted also that she was unsure Giovanni could find completeness in her incompleteness, referring to her withered leg. Giovanni admitted that it was the fire in her eyes that first interested him.

It was then that Giovanni captured the heart of Katrina. As she quizzed him about the painting before them, boasting and accrediting herself with the art, Giovanni confessed to particularly having fondness for the color of the flowers in her painting. He said, "I like the steel-blue color, as it reminds me of the color of your eyes." Katrina felt herself soften. She was falling for the son of an apothecary owner.

Katrina and her mother had their second date arranged. Giovanni was instructed to arrive at their home, dressed appropriately. He could see the lavish white stallions and carriage awaiting him as he walked toward their home.

The driver of the carriage was under instruction by Cardinal Alessandro Farnese to escort his daughter and her date. During their ride, Katrina admitted that she had chosen their first date alone, in order to show Giovanni a great portrait that reminded her of him. She said that she had often gone to the Sistine Chapel to view the art work and found that the last time she visited there, she could not help but see the similarities in the arm of the man in the "Portrait of Adam" and the arm of Giovanni's. Giovanni had never been to a museum let alone the gallery at the Sistine Chapel. Katrina placed her hand in Giovanni's on their ride home as they discussed their future life together. Gio would take over his father's apothecary and Katrina admitted that she would prefer to have a life filled with the niceties she had become accustomed to.

Giovanni and Katrina were married in 1524 in the Sant'Eustachio Cathedral in Rome. Her father officiated. He had loaned his daughter a most ornate ruby necklace, owned by the church, to wear on her wedding day. He also wanted the appearance of his daughter to reflect his lifestyle.

Following their nuptials, the same red-and-gold carriage that had driven them on their second date, escorted the newly married couple to their new home. Giovanni had taken an entire year to refurbish their home before Katrina would first view it. He carried her over the threshold. Her eyes widened and lit up as she first noticed the table for four as they entered the room, preset with formal dinnerware and ivory teacups, rimmed in gold. Katrina was ecstatic. Next, they walked into their bedroom. It had been adorned with a large, four-poster canopy bed, draped in expensive silk fabrics that lay over dark, polished wood. Giovanni was as surprised as Katrina. This was not of his doing. He would later learn that Ms. Orsini and the cardinal, Katrina's father, were responsible for the expensive décor. He had simply been responsible for refacing the older apartment. This set the tone for Katrina's expectations for her life with Giovanni.

*To be continued ...*

# Part III

# AND

## Chapter 4

# The Pod

God created order. Of course! There is more matter than antimatter, when they should be equal. Entropy or disorder should occur always, according to science. Yet, there is order and not chaos. Patterns occur spontaneously at a rate higher than probability; the formation of DNA is an example. It's improbable that DNA would form as it does. However, it does. If you stretched all the DNA in each of our cells, separately, it would be twice the diameter of the solar system. Evolution is predictable, yet it has occurred at rates above the predicted rates. Why? Because something greater has control than merely science alone.

How would God's creations interact? For, in the very beginning, all *souls*, all *Spirit Guides* and all *Angels* coexisted as one.

The energy was great but undirected. So, God created a grid; a three-dimensional framework to house and direct the energy. This grid expands in all directions, turning around and in upon itself. Imagine it like a turning, twisting and involuting infinity sign; sideways, up and down and inside out.

From a distance, it appears as an infinite number of connecting bright, white lights. Picture it as a three-dimensional ball of connecting lights. As it spins, it flattens on the north and south points. Slightly closer, you can see the lights moving around within itself, separately.

From a very great distance, you can see that it has an outer edge and an open center. You can see the outer edge become the inner circle and the inner edge become the outer circle.

You can also see that all points in the grid are, at one time, all located in the same position but constantly changing, ever moving, ever becoming.

Now, if you get much closer, you will see that the grid has no void. All spaces are filled with a uniquely stacked crystalline appearing twelve-sided Pod or capsule. Each Pod is in contact with twelve other Pods, touching together in a five-sided pentagon. In science, this is referred to as a dodecahedron. This is a twelve-sided, three-dimensional shape with no parallel sides.

Within each Pod, there are points of light presenting the energy of three souls and one Spirit Guide. Light reflects in all directions because there are no parallel sides. Therefore, the Pods receive light from twelve different directions, refracted to exactly match the spectrum of light given off by the Angels. All angles in the dodecahedron are 108 degrees. That means the light refracts differently than what most of us can perceive. We tend to perceive at 90 degrees. Therefore, each side projects a crystalline, colorful pattern within each Pod.

Human perception is 90 degrees which 90, reduced in numerology is 9. 108 degrees reduced in numerology is 9. Nine, in numerology, is as close to God as we can get; God being ten.

Because the light reflects or refracts at an unusual angle than what we would experience on Earth, those inside the Pods would describe it as un-Earthly. This means the experience in the Pod would resemble being inside a kaleidoscope. Although some have described this as appearing as being on another planet, this experience is unique only to Heaven.

Some recent scientists who are examining the universe have described the universe as having the shape of a dodecahedron.

Within each Pod there are three unique soul sisters or soul brothers. Each Pod is directly connected to twelve other Pods or thirty-six other souls. Some people would refer to this as your soul family. However, your soul family can extend to other Pods in close proximity. Therefore, your soul family is not limited to thirty-six.

Remember the involuting, turning grid; the metaphorical hole in the center? At the time of a soul's incarnation, the Pod's closest proximity is to the middle or hole of the grid returning to the Earth at the exact time. The hole is the birthplace of the soul, just as the birth canal is to the baby.

This also corresponds to the tunnel we return through, witnessed in most NDEs or near-death experiences. Why do you think you see a light at the end of the tunnel?

The Pod is impervious in all directions and points, except in the center. Therefore, we must reach the center to be released or placed once more.

It is part of God's plan that these Pods and Pods close to each other return and are incarnated together to serve two purposes. One is to support one another as family mates and the other is to serve as a karmic mate. Meaning, we are able to exist and get along as family mates, therefore, making our reincarnation easier. The other karmic mates return together for reasons of debt from a past life. They have something to achieve between each other.

The three Pod inhabitants and the Spirit Guide within each Pod have unique matching energies. They have similar qualities in character as well as expressed appearance. Their eyes could appear similarly, their mannerisms, and their health. They share similar expression of their feminine and masculine qualities.

They are not meant to be your doppelganger. They are meant to reincarnate for you in your absence. What does that mean?

It means that sometimes, maybe due to an untimely death, etc., you get off cycle and what you were meant to do is affected by yours or other's choices. For instance, let's say you incarnate to learn certain lessons. Your "intended mate" is not available to be with you to assist you in that life. A Pod brother or sister may be sent in your place to keep you on track. They are not meant to be your replacement, ever. You are always responsible for your own individual karma. In fact, it is not abnormal for your Pod sister or brother to be incarnated at the same time as you are. Why? They also reach the surface of the center at your same time. This does not mean you will know them in each reincarnation but could have the opportunity for it to happen.

While in our Pod, we contemplate our next life. We return to our Pod for that reason and to cycle back with our family mates when it is time. We have no wants or cares while in our homes/ Pods. We are protected and bathed in love.

### Isabella speaks ...

The Pod continued to involute, turning in and upon itself. The year had been 1502. A soul had reached the tunnel of incarnation. It was born under the Sign of **Aquarian.** It again turned in and upon itself. Two years later, the adjacent Pod released another soul under the Sign of **Libra.** These two family-mates seemed intended to meet. Both had been born in Rome, Italy. One was strong of arm and able to catch someone and one was weak of leg and likely to fall.

The **Aquarian** was named Giovanni by his parents and his mother had died young. The **Libra** was named Katrina and her father had been absent. This caused each of the newly reincarnated souls to be weak and strong in opposition.

This literally left both to be awkward which allowed each of them to grow in those areas together. Neither had a preconceived notion of the role they should play.

Giovanni only knew that a man provided for his wife and family. All that Katrina understood was that a man provided for his woman and children. It was easy for the hard-working **Aquarian** to provide. Yet, he had much more to learn. And, it was easy for the **Libra** to be provided for but, too, had much to learn.

Giovanni learned his very first lesson which was that he could not possibly provide everything; including that in their new home, some of the lavish furnishings were provided by his wife's parents.

Katrina very quickly learned that all of her wants could not be met as they had been in her home/POD before. The harder her husband had to work for the things *she wanted*, the less love she was bathed in. The more time and energy Giovanni spent away from Katrina, working to achieve her wants and desires, the less likely they could become in sync with one another's souls.

These two souls had been placed together without expectation and thus by their own choices were living roles which would not promote their growth individually or together. Something had to change. And shortly, thereafter, a child was born.

*To be continued ...*

## Chapter 5

# Angels

A ngels are God's action plan. They are God actually reaching out or, in other words, *the hand of God*. Each soul on Earth is assigned at least one Angel. God reaches out to everyone so that *everyone* has the hand of God.

We must spend just one moment discussing karma. Karma is being responsible for our actions and we must pay it back. Negative karma takes us farther from God. Positive karma brings us back and closer to God. Then, God literally tries to pull you back by giving you an Angel who is reaching out to you. Since karma is related to action, God gives us at least one specific Angel to help mitigate our very weakness.

Historically and biblically, there are thought to be seven *Archangels*. Angels do not vie for the limelight. They do not have pride, ego or any need or desire to be number one in God's eyes. So, Angels do not consider themselves Archangels. An Archangel by definition is an Angel of high rank. The misconception arose from misinterpretation once upon a time, long ago.

Angels do have seven legions. And, in those legions are billions of Angels. There are billions of humans, each needing an

Angel. Although there are no CEOs of the legions as we have been taught, these seven Angels have been characterized to represent the legions.

The seven Angels each have a different energy vibration. They span the spectrum of color based on their energy.

The seven colors of the spectrum are that which occur in the color of the rainbow. They range from red to purple. In the seven legions, three of the Angels carry out specific roles.

*Gabriel* – White light in color and the speaker for God and has no legion. He's the Angel of love and God's Angel. Gabriel speaks for God only. If Gabriel comes to you and speaks to you, it is directly from God.

*Michael* – Blue light in color and the protector of God. Yet, God needs no protection. Michael had a legion of three. Michael is God's warrior and destroyer. Some religions believe that a Satan or a fallen Angel has control over people's actions and can cause them to sin or act negatively.

The actual story starts with the three Angels questioning after God had made all souls, giving them a choice. Although these three Angels were the warriors for God, they decided that choice was a more powerful weapon. God then gave them choice and the three Angels decided to leave God. God instructed Estes to remove their names from THE *METAPHORICAL* BOOK and banished them from his/her presence until which time all souls return back to Heaven. This did not mean they were banished forever but just until all souls are back in God's presence. The three Angels cannot fathom time without God and they immediately realized their loss and felt the absence of God. Michael protects the three outcasted Angels. He prays with them daily to get all souls back to Heaven so they can go back to God. He maintains God's plan. Michael's great strength comes from God. He shares his great strength as a gift from God to focus God's energy and light to those who provide spiritual healing such as Reiki.

**\*Estes** – Royal purple light in color and the scribe of God. The Angel of God's BOOK. Estes has written every soul's Angel and Spirit Guide's name in THE BOOK from the start. He does not have a legion of Angels. When the three Angels were banished, God had Estes remove their names from THE BOOK. He is sometimes called Metatron. At the moment a name is recorded in THE BOOK, it is the start of what some people refer to as the Akashic record.

■　■　■

There are four remaining legions of Angels, each represented by a color and represented by the following Angel names in no particular order.

Each color is representative of an action related to past karma. This does not necessarily mean you have that same tendency in this life but could. God gives you the Angel of that tendency to help you overcome it. Those tendencies are *conceit, selfishness, jealousy* and *unforgiveness*.

**Raphael** – Green in color. Also, the Angel of peaceful relationships. The green color is representative of jealousy. It is associated with the astrological signs of Leo, Virgo and Libra.

If you are jealous in any relationship, you are only thinking of yourself. It is about relationships being more peaceful and giving of yourself in all ways.

**Uriel** – Red in color. The Angel of *right* thought. The red color is representative of unforgiveness. It is associated with the astrological signs of Scorpio, Sagittarius and Capricorn.

Uriel is present at every Atonement; Atonement meaning reconciliation with God after a life on Earth. You must forgive everyone and everything. Unforgiveness is self-destructive.

**Mariel** – Yellow in color. The Angel of healing. The yellow color is representative of selfishness. It is associated with the astrological signs of Aquarius, Pisces and Aries.

It's about giving of yourself. It's a more mental, inward desire. Don't hold onto things. Physically or mentally. Selfishness tends to be self-destructive.

**Chamuel** – Pink in color. The Angel of beautiful thoughts. The pink color is representative of conceit. It is associated with the astrological signs of Taurus, Gemini and Cancer.

We are all special, no one is more special in any way than another. Conceit is more physical, as … I think I am more special and entitled.

■  ■  ■

While meditating it is possible to see colors that appear differently than your astrological sign color. Follow your sign color. The explanation is simple. The spectrum of light blends together. All Angels vibrate above the color (or level) of purple. Thus, purple can blend together with their related color and form a new or different color. It is also possible for us to have additional Angels through our lifetimes which correspond to other colors. This is God specifically helping us in an area we are struggling with.

■  ■  ■

Next is a crude color chart with corresponding Angels and astrological signs. You will find the weakness or past-life karmic trait associated with the Angel and sign.

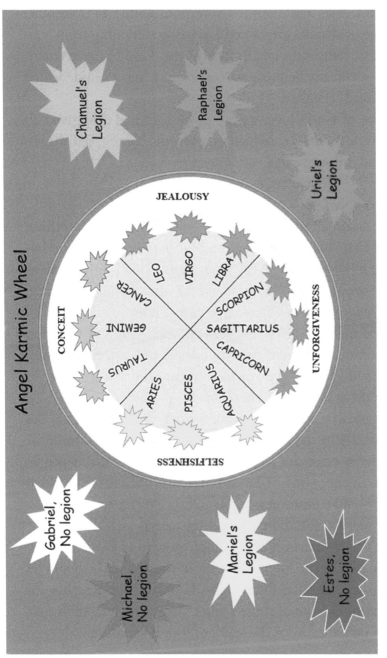

# Angel Karmic Wheel

JEALOUSY

CONCEIT

UNFORGIVENESS

SELFISHNESS

LEO · VIRGO · LIBRA · CANCER · SCORPION · GEMINI · SAGITTARIUS · TAURUS · CAPRICORN · ARIES · PISCES · AQUARIUS

Chamuel's Legion

Raphael's Legion

Uriel's Legion

Gabriel, No legion

Michael, No legion

Mariel's Legion

Estes, No legion

**If viewing this chart in black-and-white print,**

Gabriel is white; Estes is purple; Michael is blue; Mariel is yellow – Aries, Pisces, Aquarius; Chamuel is pink – Taurus, Gemini, Cancer; Raphael is green – Leo, Virgo, Libra; Uriel is red – Scorpio, Sagittarius, Capricorn

God did this on purpose? Yes, we are born under a sign with specific tendencies and qualities to test our ability to overcome. So, the four tendencies are *all* and *everything* stemming from conceit, jealousy, selfishness and unforgiveness. God has given us an Angel to specifically help us overcome and a Spirit Guide which we have already detailed.

Because of God's love, we are given help and also given an Angel in the form of love, to help us overcome conceit, selfishness, jealousy and unforgiveness.

### The Angels speak ...

Many assume that I only speak when God has something to say and that this happens few and far between. Yet, God has something to be said, every day. You assume that I only speak to important people; however, it is that you only listen to *so-called* important people. All of you are special and none of you are more special. God speaks to all of you, daily through your Spirit Guides. They are unique to you as you are unique to God. Sometimes, God speaks louder because you cannot hear the whisper. This is not out of anger but rather out of love.

If you ask why, it is that I speak to you, it is because I am the *Angel* of *Love*. Why did I speak to Henry before he was Giovanni? Because, Henry could not reconcile being a ruler and taking people into battle in the name of love. Therefore, Henry was guided into the arts and education as a way to express love to his people. And, why every night, did Giovanni fall asleep with the thought of Katrina's steel-blue eyes and a single thought of love? Because, I reminded him of the fire he first saw in those eyes. It should be of no surprise then, that some nights Giovanni and Katrina did not fall asleep. On one of those nights, they conceived their first daughter, Gabriella ... for the spark of love is creation.

*Love, Gabriel* (meaning: **God is my strength**)

■ ■ ■

I have recorded many names. Including the names that mean …
*God is my Oath, Lioness of God, Beloved, Beautiful Flower,* and including … Gabriella, meaning … *God is my Strength.* All of you have
been listed, named and recorded.

This is a metaphorical book because, really, you are listed in
God's heart. Just as your children should be a spark of your love,
you are a spark of God's.

*Love, Estes* (**Scribe of God**)

■ ■ ■

They had so much love, yet Giovanni was unsure how much
more he could give. As Gio worked long hours and grew tired, he
angered. To anger while giving is a sign of selfishness.

My legion is that of healing. It took but a small reminder to
Giovanni that life was about Ahav and Ahava; which is to love and
give without expectation. Giovanni was born as an **Aquarian** for
just this moment of selfishness.

*Love, Mariel* (**the Angel of healing**)

■ ■ ■

They had so much love, yet Katrina could not see what she already
had. Katrina had a conflict between what she had and what she
wanted. This put stress on what should have been a peaceful relationship. Soon, a gold-rimmed teacup would hit the floor.

Giovanni and Katrina's first daughter, Gabriella, was around
the age of four when she walked into their dining room table,

accidentally knocking one of the gold-rimmed teacups to the floor. It shattered into pieces. Katrina yelled in anger, "Gabriella, that teacup cannot be replaced!" Gabriella began to cry, uncontrollably. Giovanni ran to comfort their daughter, immediately. He then said, "Katrina, it was just a teacup. If you want, I can work even longer hours to buy another teacup but you will miss me when I'm gone!" Katrina spun around in anger, losing her balance as her crutch gave way. Giovanni was there to catch her as he always had been. He said, "Katrina, I will always be there for you when you fall but this will not be the only time one of our girls will fall, and YOU will need to catch them." Giovanni's words touched Katrina. She felt ashamed and now understood his words and the importance of the love she had for her husband and their daughter. As she crawled across the floor toward her daughter it changed both her and Giovanni. Giovanni saw that it was more important that Katrina reach her daughter than keeping her pride held up with a crutch.

On that day, Gio's Angel of healing and Katrina's Angel of peaceful relationships were both present. Both Giovanni and Katrina softened and their love grew.

**Love, *Raphael* (the Angel of peaceful relationships)**

*To be continued ...*

■   ■   ■

*Back to the Twelves ...*

But why are there *Twelve* astrological signs, we ask? First of all, we do not always come back under the same sign. This is planned. Different signs display different tendencies and characteristics along with your environment. God tests us to find out whether we have truly learned from our past lives.

*Twelve* appears to be a common denominator throughout life because God chose the dodecahedron, the *Twelve*-sided, three-dimensional, five pentagon-faced shape, for the universe and for the souls' very first home. Therefore, there was no void or emptiness in the grid. Thus, God created the astrological system to represent *Twelve* faces of humanity. The *Twelve* faces were represented in the Heavens or sky. Therefore, man divided the cycle of the rotation around the sun into *Twelve* parts or months. Then, man divided the day into night and day, originally *Twelve* hours of day and *Twelve* hours of night. And again, as man defined length, the length of the average foot became *Twelve* inches. A standard quantity of a commodity became a dozen (or *Twelve*). When early man tried to define himself, he developed *Twelve* archetypes. In other words, a soul must progress through lessons that are based on *Twelve*; *Twelve* archetypes, *Twelve* zodiac signs or *Twelve* traits that we will introduce to you soon along with the archetypes.

And speaking of *Twelves*, the number *Twelve* carries mythological, religious and magical symbolism, representing perfection, entirety or cosmic order in traditions, since forever. The Bible had *Twelve* Tribes of Israel and *Twelve* Apostles; there are *Twelve* donuts in a dozen; in ancient Greek religion there were *Twelve* Olympians; there are *Twelve* days of Christmas; in Greek mythology, the Goddess Athena summons *Twelve* citizens to sit on the first jury; in Hinduism there are *Twelve* self-formed Lingas of Lord Shiva in Hindu temples; in the legend of King Arthur, he is said to have subdued *Twelve* rebel princes to win *Twelve* great battles, there were *Twelve* Imams or legitimate successors to the prophet Muhammad. We suggest you google the stories behind most of these for significance. Is it a coincidence that the human body has *Twelve* cranial nerves? *Twelve* is the number of full lunations of the moon in a year, and the number of years for a full cycle of Jupiter.

Each astrological sign has its own strengths and weaknesses. Each archetype has its own lesson. Each trait comes with karma.

So, therefore, each soul could be placed in a sign, an archetype and a trait that teaches, challenges and strengthens our ability to overcome conceit, jealousy, selfishness and unforgiveness. If that is not enough help … God then gives us an Angel and Spirit Guides at our side to help us whether we know it or not.

## Chapter 6

# Originals

M any of us have already figured out, Adam and Eve could not have been the only couple planted on the Earth in the beginning. Why? Because, their children would not have had suitable partners, outside of incest.

Here is our Spirit Guide's explanation on the evolutionary process of woman and man: *Ye who carries the water; ye who carries the vessel.*

In the beginning, the human had to evolve to a high enough level to make choices about the welfare of others and not just about the welfare of themselves. This human could now understand the consequences of their actions. Remember, the soul would be placed in a human once it realized understanding and consequences, thus, a storage place for understanding and consequences was then necessary.

Thus, the human form became the learning ground of the soul. And, the soul became the location of the lessons learned and the depository for karmic debt.

We've been informed by our Spirit Guides, all original souls were placed in humans over a twelve-year period, starting approximately 6,000 years ago. All of the *Original* couples were uniquely matched to each other, distributed and born across heavily inhabited areas of the Homo sapiens population. Each *Original* couple was born into the same tribe or social unit to ensure that they would recognize a like-spirit in each other's eyes. This drew the *Original* couples together as there could be no like-spirit in the eyes of the other members.

The first soul was placed in the middle east during the Hebrew month of Shevat which was under the sign of Aquarius. This is important, as Aquarius is the sign of the vessel who carries the water. Thus, literally, the first female was born under the sign of the vessel that carries the water that carries life. The first male, born hours later but within the same day, was born in the Hebrew month of Adar under the sign of Pisces. Literally meaning, he carries the life force that swims, Pisces being the sign of the fish. *God first placed a soul in woman and said, "You will be inspiration, creation, the Tree of Life, strength and beauty, both. You will bear the future." God then placed a soul in man and said, "You will be her love, vitality, partner and equal; complete, only together." Together the two will possess wisdom, they do not have apart.*

Woman holds half the seed in the vessel to which a life is carried and man holds the other half of the seed to complete the life in the vessel. Although men and women create the human being, it is God who places the soul. Interestingly enough, this was not the case with all the *Original* couples but in the first *Original* couple, God gradually placed twelve new little souls.

God always has a plan. However, human choices always have an effect on those plans. The first *Original* couple had twelve children; each born under a different astrological sign.

God's plan was, in all the *Original* localities, to equally distribute, the twelve astrological sign births, therefore, giving the Earth all blends of personalities in the first humans. Thus, each family unit would have a mixture of all personalities, weaknesses and strengths; learning from each other, supporting each other and complementing each other.

But human choice is not controllable. The distribution of signs was not always equal. Some *Original* couples had few children and others had many children leaving the opportunities for matchmaking limited; therefore, also limiting the choices of compatibility in astrological signs. God attempted to alleviate the incompatibility by distributing the astrological signs as equally as possible in births to these *Original* couples.

Sign compatibility may stay reasonably balanced. However, age compatibility may not be. The astrological sign of a Libra ready to be connected to a compatible sign from another social unit, may not have the age compatible with the sign compatibility. Perhaps the compatible sign of Aries was an infant and not anywhere ready to bond as a couple to the Libra. Thus, the first true human conflict is the search for a compatible soul. It is still true today.

The gift of a compatible mate was first given to the *Originals* by God. In reality, God has provided still today the tools to assist in our quest for a compatible mate by giving us astrological signs. So, consider the first *Original* couple. Both were born on the cusp of an astrological sign. They each possessed the qualities of both signs, Aquarian and Pisces. Therefore, they had both similar and different characteristics about themselves. Thus, they were stronger than either would have been alone. It was always meant to be. It was God's help and plan.

■　　■　　■

Let's visit the subject of reincarnation again. A soul returns to Earth often with assistance, prearranged, with our *primary soul group*, called by some. This is comprised of two separate sets of souls. Again, there are the karmic-mates and the family-mates. Family-mates are those we feel comfortable with, work well with and get assistance and support within our growth. That is the reason we would choose, together with God, to have them return to Earth with us. Second, our karmic-mates are those we are encouraged to return with because we have created negative karma with each other. The karmic cause is by either one or both of us.

We are guided in our choices by our Spirit Guides and Counsel, although we have a limited amount of choices, the decisions are ultimately not ours but rather God's. So, let us confirm so we all understand completely, our Spirit Guides help us to make choices about reincarnating but the final choice belongs to God and only God. The purpose of reincarnation is for us to evolve and grow; if we do not make the choices that will allow for our growth, we will be guided firmly to make those choices.

If we did not have assistance with our choices, reincarnation would be endless. We are guided with choices so that we will make conscious, *free-will* decisions, during each lifetime which directly affect our karma. This can lead to additional karma or healing of our karma. If there was no assistance, we would all choose to come back as millionaires, in perfect health, skipping through life on easy street and what would we learn from that?

Even if we were given that perfect life, did we make decisions based on love or were they based on selfishness, jealousy, conceit and unforgiveness?

Love is a challenge. First, because it cannot exist with selfishness, conceit, jealousy and unforgiveness.

Love in a relationship is not simply romantic. Love exists in friendships, families, work places and in a couple. And, karma exists within all of these types of relationships.

We can say that we are not selfish in our relationships but are we patient? Are we resistant to change?

We can say that we are not jealous in our relationships. But are we insecure, never satisfied and always worried about what we want?

We can also say that we are not conceited but are we stubborn and always want our own way believing our way is the only way?

We can say that we are forgiving but are we actually angry and self-destructive? Not forgiving ourselves or others is being unforgiving.

The karma created with these emotions helps God, Counsel and our Spirit Guides choose which astrological sign and trait we will be born into. Conceit, jealousy, selfishness and unforgiveness must be overcome. Karma that must be overcome could include abuse, disability, failure, injustice, loss, addiction, intolerance and/or abandonment. You either inflicted or had something to do with the infliction of these conditions on another soul in a previous life.

■　　■　　■

We have all heard conflicting terminology related to whether one specific soul is meant for another. They have been referred to as twin flames, soulmates, life partners to name a few. God had a plan from the beginning to provide each soul with the perfect mate. We refer to those partners as our *"Intendeds"* meaning they were always intended to be together. *Intendeds* were created to uniquely complement each other, not to complete one another.

*Intendeds* are much like the concept of twin flames. However, we each have our own soul. A soul is never shared or split because we are each responsible for our own karma. No one shares our choices or actions. We each have our own depository for karma which is our soul. And, the Akashic record is nothing more than a metaphor for the soul.

Our happiness is not dependent on meeting our *Intended*. Because, our *Intended* may not be present in every one of our lives. Our *Intended* may not even be available as a love interest. For example, they may be our parent or sibling during one of our lifetimes, coming to assist us in that particular life, not for us to find romantic love. However, our *Intended* is always part of our family mates (or soul group).

There is a specific trait in humans (traits, we will discuss later) which is based on karma between two *Intendeds*. This is called the Crystal trait. If the karma is not released between the *Intended* Crystals after however many lifetimes, then the *Intendeds* can be released. If the Crystal *Intendeds* continue to judge each other through conceited, selfish, jealous and unforgiving eyes they will be released as *Intendeds*. This does not imply that two *Intended* Crystals could not overcome their karma with love. The shame is that there is no greater attraction or better match than with *Intendeds*. And, all of the *Originals* (we discussed before) were, indeed, *Intendeds*.

Implying the word twin in twin flame suggests that one soul can split into two. This is not possible. Implying the word flame suggests that God created something that could be burned out. It is our reaction to our humanity that burns out any flame. Saying that there is a split soul implies that one half is incomplete. God creates no souls to be incomplete. Being a twin flame should almost be offensive. It implies that we could not be complete without that other side.

Soulmates have been described in many ways. So, there is no confusion, all *Intendeds* do not become soulmates. In fact, it is possible to become a soulmate but not have been an *Intended*. How is this possible?

What is a soulmate? Soulmates are two individual souls who so complemented each other through many lives together, that God invited them after their final reincarnation to become one, emulating God in completeness. This does not happen until each soul is finished. Often, the souls finish at different times, not together, since they are not always incarnated together. God asks each soul, separately, if they would choose to be one with that other soul. The choice again is ours. These souls so perfected their love for one another that God uses them as an example of divine love.

■　■　■

How did God design each of us? First, we were placed in a unique twelve-sided Pod with two like souls and a Spirit Guide, immediately adjacent to twelve other Pods. This gave us an immediate soul family of thirty-nine. This does not include the Spirit Guides.

Remembering that each Pod is attached by twelve sides that, therefore, extends the outer soul family to 468. This is a three-dimensional framework so, in fact, all of us are connected.

The unique dodecahedron represents the shape of each Pod and the Universe; stacked upon itself with no void. Each side is a pentagon representing the twelve faces of humanity. These are also representative of the twelve astrological signs, the twelve traits and the twelve archetypes.

God incarnates us intentionally under a certain astrological sign, a certain trait and a certain archetype designed to aid us in growth along our path back to home. If that doesn't seem sufficiently intricate, God will modify those three characteristics with the most basic of elementals which are air, earth, water and fire.

These are not in any particular order or list, nor do they correspond necessarily with what is next to them. These are just a list of the twelve types of Signs, Traits and Archetypes.

| Sign | Trait | Archetype |
| --- | --- | --- |
| Aquarius | Warm | Magician |
| Pisces | Crystal | Orphan |
| Aries | Rainbow | Creator |
| Taurus | Esoteric Highness | Innocent |
| Gemini | Camel's Hump | Sage |
| Cancer | Willow | Lover |
| Leo | Elephant | Jester |
| Virgo | Squirrel | Rebel |
| Libra | Loon | Caregiver |
| Scorpio | Anteater | Hero |
| Sagittarius | Owl | Explorer |
| Capricorn | Mother Bull | Ruler |

# The Signs ... What is Written in the Stars

A ll *Astrological Signs* are necessary in the world, to function cohesively. Although it may appear that some signs are more easy going or more driven, each and every sign is essential and has a purpose. Although it may appear the following explanations of each *Astrological Sign* are critical and/or negative, these are written in regard to karmic issues. Please, do not take offense or feel badly for incarnating under a certain sign. These are gifts from God to assist you on your path or growth and evolution.

*Astrological Signs* have been observed by nearly all religions and cultures over time.

Astrology, historically has been studied by the Greeks, Romans, Mayans, Aztecs, Chinese, Egyptians, the Jewish believing in Kabbalah, the Essenes, Enoch a Jewish Scholar and Prophet, Druids, Celtics, Wiccans, Hindus and is mentioned in many works of literature such as William Shakespeare, Dante Alighieri, Geoffrey Chaucer, Lope de Vega, Calderon de le Barca. Kings and Queens have used astrology over the centuries and went so far as to have a court astrologer. The astrologer would be consulted on many issues from when to enter a battle to when to be crowned, and who to marry and who to trust.

Roman Caesar and Alfred the Great used astrology to assist in their lives. Charlemagne used an astrologer. William the Conqueror and Henry II were tutored by astrologers. Sir Isaac Newton was a practicing astrologer, as was Nostradamus. Stonehenge was aligned with the stars, sun and moon and was considered an early form of astrology.

The Abbey of Glastonbury, a monastery in England, actually had the zodiac set into their floor. The Medieval monks of the Abbey invented the site (after the story had been created of Arthur and Guinevere) of King Arthur's tomb in the year 1101 to draw visitors to raise money. This way, they were able to convert the myth into money. A fire had destroyed the Abbey.

The symbol of Jesus is known as the fish. Because Jesus was actually born under the sign of Pisces. Most likely, he was born during this time with baby lambs attending his birth, as the story is told, which we know are born in early spring not winter.

One of the oldest known religions, Zoroastrians believed in and used astrology in their teachings.

Human observation of the position of the stars has been used to define personality traits of the zodiac. However, the position of the stars does not determine these characteristics. These characteristics were created by God to aid us in finding a suitable partner in life and to challenge us in our growth. The sky does not influence the signs, but just happens to be observed in their position at the time of our births.

■　■　■

We'll begin with **Aquarius** since the first soul born 6,000 years ago was under the sign of the water bearer. *Aquarius* starts in the third week of January to the third week of February and is an air sign which we will discuss later. They carry a masculine pull or polarity.

Those born under the sign of *Aquarius* have a unique combination of masculine and feminine qualities. And, *Aquarians* are comfortable with both of those qualities. They encompass a strong, independent spirit with the need to be free of restrictions and conventional ideas. They are inclined to think outside the box. *Aquarians* are on a quest of self-discovery. They are nonconformists yet they follow what they believe is right, living by those principles. The water bearers are hard-working and drawn to humanitarian issues which makes them deeply upset with injustice and oppression. *Aquarian* women are strongly attuned to people and the Earth. Although they are fighters for the underdog, they possess a more vulnerable character than they would make known. *Aquarians* tend to be extremely loyal to friends and family and expect the same in return.

*Aquarians'* independence can be confused with being aloof, distant or disinterested. Thinking outside the box can be misconstrued as being unconventional. Their strength is often misread as being bossy, because they are. Standing up for their beliefs often causes discord on behalf of those who are unyielding and often makes the *Aquarian* appear to be unyielding; which goes along with their knack for impatience. *Aquarians* are sometimes quick to act and slow to evaluate, however, that speaks to the passion of their character.

*Aquarians* are compatible with all air signs and feminine polarity signs.

Abraham Lincoln, an *Aquarian*, fought for a cause and slavery. With his strong personality, it's no wonder he pulled off the Emancipation Proclamation that freed slaves. Galileo, Thomas Edison and Charles Darwin, all *Aquarians*, thought outside the box in the science and invention world. Galileo got in trouble with the church when he agreed that we were not the center of the Universe. If not for Thomas Edison, we couldn't get a true picture of ourselves. Charles Darwin championed evolution in nature and our soul which evolves as part of nature.

Franklin D. Roosevelt, an *Aquarian*, was the first American president to be televised. Now, we can't get the presidents to stay in their office and stay off social media. Rosa Parks and Susan B. Anthony both strong, independent *Aquarian* women, stood up proudly for their beliefs. These are all examples of the *Aquarian* capabilities.

The greatest fear for the *Aquarian* is change, which can lead to paralysis. Emotional loss can also lead the *Aquarian* to paralysis. The third and fourth fears are death (which is change) and self-sacrifice which leads nowhere. In all actuality, these four fears are very tied to one another and could suspiciously resemble selfishness.

■ ■ ■

**Pisces**-born persons have a pull or polarity of the feminine nature. They are a water sign (go figure, the fish) and are compatible with other water signs as well as those with a masculine polarity. The sign starts in February and goes into mid-March.

*Pisceans* tend to be sensitive and have deep intuition as well as much emotion. They display a strong sense of empathy for everyone and everything along with kindness and compassion. Their minds are emotional sponges which could cause them to tire emotionally and physically, needing time to rest in private. There are times when the *Pisces*-born will sit on a line between being an introvert or an extrovert, pulling them into different directions. It is also true that the *Piscean* can sit on the line between the spiritual and the worldly. They are full of love, romance and creativity which gives them the potential for great joy and lasting happiness.

The *Piscean*, being very emotional, does not always admit to it. *Pisceans* are very susceptible to outside influences and tend to allow themselves insecurity which can pull them into their introverted self. They are slow to face reality often in relationships even when it is obvious and apparent to everyone else, and normally occurs in their less-mature stages of life. Because they have a significant ability to absorb information, they sometimes become confused by all the choices available and must think on it for a while. Often that leads to no decision at all.

*Pisceans* attempt to see the best side of everyone they encounter, however, that makes them a bit too trusting in a potentially bad situation. They are not materialistic and follow their heart. They are extremely selfless and idealistic. A *Piscean* born is calm in the storm.

Mr. Rogers, a *Piscean*, is liked by everyone in the neighborhood. Elizabeth Taylor, a *Piscean*, apparently engaged her romantic side over and over again.

George Washington, also a *Piscean*, was a terrific people-person and gave confidence to all those around him as the founding father of America and he did father a lot of America. Cyrano de Bergerac proved his ability for romance and selflessness as a *Piscean*, despite the nose on his face.

Another well-known *Piscean* Edgar Cayce opened up his mind and a can of worms with his mystical information. Lou Costello, another *Piscean*, couldn't make up his mind as to who was on which base.

And, Theodore Geisel, another *Piscean* and otherwise known as Dr. Seuss, made a lot of children laugh with happiness while living in his fantasy land. These are the capabilities of *Piscean*-born people.

The *Piscean* fears loss of love most of all; all kinds of lost love feels painful. Then in a close second, third and fourth place, they fear lack of change and inertia, death and self-sacrifice without results. Again, could the *Piscean* be displaying selfishness?

■  ■  ■

**Aries**-born persons, under the fire element, have typically been at the beginning of the astrology chart due to the onset of spring in the northern hemisphere. Their sign (the ram) begins in March going through until the middle of April. They are known to be natural-born leaders; however, it appears to be due to their aggression, egotism and stubbornness. They do, indeed, have a determined spirit ... to get their own way. They believe their way is the best way. *Ariens* require outside activities for action, adventure and to appease their daring nature. Their need to win and compete go hand and hand with their belief of being first not only in astrology but also in everything. Their concerns regarding their own vitality are part of their egotism. Gutsy and impulsive, their reactions and decisions often appear to turn out well.

Believed to be the infant of the zodiac, *Ariens* tend to dismiss the feelings of others, selfishly ignoring the needs of those others. *Aries*-born persons are enthusiastic and curious, never having a dull moment in life. Perseverance a.k.a. impatience tends to surface without stimulation. But, if you want a job done, hire the *Aries* and they'll succeed, but only if they want to. Remember, nothing will actually happen without the *Ariens'* focus and discipline.

The *Aries* person has a great sense of humor and attempts to get the most from their lives. However, when disappointed the *Ariens* become disillusioned, unmotivated, withdrawn and furious. The nearest available target is sure to reap those benefits. *Ariens* fall under the masculine polarity.

Thomas Jefferson, born an *Aries*, was the third president of the United States and best known for his independence in marriage, keeping his slave-girlfriend, regardless.

William Booth, a well-respected *Aries*, was best known for his founding of the Salvation Army; it was his second-hand choice. Heath Ledger, also born under the sign of *Aries* was best known for his acting abilities and being quite the joker.

King Henry IV of England was born under the sign of *Aries*. He switched from being Protestant to Catholic to secure his marriage and his kingdom over France. But, in the end, he met his demise by a Catholic fanatic. The grass was not greener. He should have stayed who he was.

The next *Aries* is Maya Angelou (Marguerite Annie Johnson) best known as a poet, and we all know it. "Do the best you can until you know better, then when you know better, do better."

Pete Rose born under the *Aries* sign is best known for his athletic ability in baseball. He took a gamble on life and finally won.

Vincent van Gogh was best known for his artistic talent and also born as an *Aries*. He was starry, starry eyed for painting! These are examples of the capabilities of the *Aries* person.

The fear with *Aries* lies first in self-sacrifice. Death scares the *Aries* almost to death! Then, lack of change and inertia because of it and, finally, loss of anything. That's selfishness.

■　　■　　■

Those born under the sign of the **Taurus** or the bull, or the earth sign, begin their days in April, ending in mid-May. *Taurus* has a feminine polarity or pull.

A *Taurus* has an artistic flair, is strong-willed and appears to be rather down to Earth. However, there is a need for material wealth although possessing practicality. *Taureans* are obstinately resistant to change which can lead to displays of anger when their plans are crossed. This brings about their need for a regular rhythm in their daily life. They are also solid and dependable. Their natural sense of justice can also lead them to condemn those who do not agree with their thinking or ways.

Their pride, determination and self-confidence must not be beaten by demanding challenges or else the *Taurean* will become obsessed in their pursuits, convincing them of their stress and overwork. A solid relationship is very important to the *Taurus* person along with a stable home and fulfilling job. They can be quite compassionate but tend to be overly authoritative.

Once the *Taurean* has set their mind on achieving a goal, nothing will get in their way. A common-sense approach to life is their way of leaving drama and turmoil which go against their nature. The *Taurus* person is extremely strong physically and can work for long hours without tiring. Many *Taureans* have issues maintaining their weight with a sluggish metabolism and tendency to overeat. Resting and taking it easy comes naturally to those born under the *Taurus* sign.

Golda Meir, a born *Taurus,* was a successful prime minister and greatly admired throughout her life. All that glitters is Golda. Ulysses S. Grant led the Northern troops during the Civil War, also a *Taurus.* He never took for Grant-ed that the North would win.

Another well-known *Taurus* was James Madison, the fifth president of the United States who wrote the Monroe Doctrine which was intolerance to European influence in the United States. We wonder if the Europeans can tolerate Dolly Madison cakes?

The famous singer and dancer James Brown, felt **very good** as a *Taurus.* Another famous singer who believed she should **stand by her man,** was Tammy Wynette although she eventually divorced her man.

John Wilkes Booth may not have been the most-liked *Taurus* after making fame with the shooting and death of our President Abraham Lincoln with his whole world becoming a stage.

Bea Arthur made her claim to fame as a *Taurus* and as Dorothy in the *Golden Girls;* her thoughts were quite Maud-ern. All are *Taureans;* some known with positivity, some not.

The *Taurus* sign fears inferiority more than anything else! Next, the feeling of powerlessness brings great fear and then, going hand in hand, their fear of authority for anyone other than themselves. Lastly, they fear loss of self-control. Sounds like conceit.

■ ■ ■

An air sign, the **Gemini** starts in the third week of May and ends in the third week of June. A masculine pull or polarity, they are highly restless and need constant stimulation of their brain. They tend to bore easily, needing a wide array of experiences to dull the tedium.

*Geminis* are very social by nature and love communicating with others, never lacking in conversation. Their quick mind loves knowledge and acquires it easily. Their tendency toward the intellectual leads to an egotistical mindset. They have inherent self-confidence and self-belief. However, it causes difficulty in them admitting to their own personal failings.

They are called the twins for a reason. Their duality and complexity speak to the need for constant contrast and change. *Geminis* love to keep busy and possess a nervous energy. *Geminis* love children and children seem to be drawn to them as well.

The *Gemini's* need for adventure may lead to danger. The constant need for stimulation could lead to flirting and other adventures outside their relationship. *Geminis* require an active social life and going along with the active social life, they love fashion and the latest trends. This makes the *Gemini* difficult to settle down. *Geminis* love to live near the action and love the hustle and bustle of a larger city.

The *Gemini* person finds it difficult to hold onto money and loves spending it especially on all the various expeditions they are inclined to take.

They have a natural inclination to lead others; however, this tends to make them a bit too domineering. *Geminis* feel trapped when being forced to have too many commitments as they like to make their own choices and keep open for all possibilities.

George H.W. Bush was our forty-first president and a *Gemini*. He was a vicious opponent to Bill Clinton and then the other half of the *Gemini* decided to become Bill's friend. John F. Kennedy, a

*Gemini* and the thirty-fifth president of our United States led the country all the while being greatly admired, especially by good-looking female actresses.

Anne Frank was a *Gemini* and well known for passing her days writing her diary, hiding, during the second World War. Let's be frank, we couldn't have withstood what she had to endure.

The Marquis de Sade, a well-known *Gemini,* was best known for his writing of erotica; we wonder if he felt chained and tied to his typewriter?

Marilyn Monroe, another famous *Gemini,* although fashionable and loved by many (especially men), after all was said and done, diamonds really were her best friends. Judy Garland, also a *Gemini,* was very demanding, especially of herself which eventually did take her over the rainbow. Nicole Kidman, a *Gemini,* is a well-respected actress also and known for her love of fashion and choosing to live the Urban life.

These are examples of *Geminis* not necessarily all functioning at their highest level but also examples of some who rose above.

*Geminis* fear loss of self-control the most. The flip side of the *Gemini* twin especially fears the feeling of inferiority to anyone. Powerlessness is next and the fear of authority comes in close to that. However, in the case of the *Gemini,* all of these four fears, actually blend into one another. These fears are all four related to conceit.

■　■　■

**Cancer** is a feminine polarity or pull and is also a water sign. The crab likes water! They appear to be strong and tough, but are rather sensitive and vulnerable. *Cancer* signs start in the third week of June and end in the third week of July.

*Cancers* possess many wonderful qualities such as loyalty, sensitivity and intuition and are nurturing and protective as well. Although very moody and withdrawn at times, the *Cancerian* has very delicate emotions having the need to feel safe. This withdrawal can be within self or with the use of mind altering or food substances.

Family and friends are very important to the *Cancer*, holding them near and dear. Being very attached to the past, the *Cancer* person can miss opportunities in the present while dwelling in that past. Almost psychic in their ability, they can pick up on people's feelings and the on-goings in their minds. *Cancer's* complex nature and changing moods are sometimes a bit too much to deal with. They often sabotage their own best interests. The *Cancer* requires security at home and in the bank account to be at ease in life.

The *Cancer* has a real flair for creation and design with their highly imaginative talent. They also have a strong feel for self-preservation which guides in their decision-making.

*Cancers* are humanitarian and altruistic, easily upset over nature, the environment, natural and man-made disasters. This tends to create negativity and pessimism.

They benefit from regular exercise to help them relax and counter their anxiety. *Cancers* work best with routine and stay happier within it.

The *Cancer* is very cautious with money matters. This goes hand and hand with the need to hold on to what they have, making them smart and shrewd with money.

*Cancers*, being very emotional, have a tendency to affect their immune system through their feelings. Depression will not only affect them mentally but also physically. Digestion is impaired in the *Cancer* whose mental state is not healthy.

Nelson Mandala, born a *Cancer*, was an antiapartheid activist and South African president who received the Nobel Peace Prize for his efforts. Helen Keller overcame many obstacles with blindness, also a *Cancer*, being the first blind person to receive a bachelor of arts degree. Wonder if her second degree was in pinball?

The fourteenth Dali Lama, Tenzin Gyatso, was born a *Cancer* and chose exile from his country to advocate for the welfare of Tibetans, teaching Buddhism. He's been known to hang with both officers and gentlemen. These are wonderful examples of perseverance and overcoming.

Robin Williams, also a *Cancer*, was well-known for making people laugh as a famous comedian but his last act left the world in tears. A well-known writer, Ernest Hemmingway, also a *Cancer*, could simply not be happy, finally hearing his **bell toll** at the end.

Princess Diana Spencer, a *Cancer*, was loved by all with compassion for everything and everyone, except for herself. She was happy, then was sad, being quite the Camilla, we mean chameleon, just to get through life.

*Cancer*-born sisters and newspaper columnists Ann Landers and Dear Abby, in all their wisdom and intuitiveness, were not afraid to give their opinions.

*Cancer* fears authority believing they somehow know more than most! Powerlessness is feared because they would hate to lose self-control. Inferiority is their fourth cause for alarm. Conceit is not just looking in the mirror. Conceit is presuming to be smarter than others.

■   ■   ■

**Leo** the lion is born under the masculine polarity or pull, and is another fire sign. *Leos* are self-possessed thus finding it difficult to let others have their say. The lion sign is energetic, courageous and strong but intellectually independent with too much (lion) pride. Unfortunately, this can cause, egotism, vanity and self-indulgence.

Once setting their mind to something, the *Leo* is very determined. They feel like they are the king of the jungle and demand respect, not necessarily being earned. Although they desire love and affection from everyone, if not the result, they will trample on anyone getting in their way. If able to calm their actions, their kind and generous heart can be detected.

*Leos* cannot fathom submitting to the authority of anyone. They are the king! *Leos* are charming, confident and used to getting their own way. They have a need for attention and the need to be adored by their audience.

Fantastic willpower is an attribute of the *Leo* giving them a tremendous chance at succeeding in their endeavors. Although relaxed by nature the majority of the time, when the *Leos* lose their temper, it can be frightening!

*Leos* are very proud and love to make their home as spectacular and homey as possible, loving the attention it could bring. They will make their home as palatial as their budget will allow and may find it difficult to tighten their belt when necessary and go as far as to borrow funds to enable their lavish lifestyle.

Their strong constitution means the *Leo* is negligent about caring for their health. The *Leo* does not prefer to appear weak or ill at health although they love the attention gained by illness.

*Leos* are great leaders but tend to be very suspicious of others offering help in any way. They will work hard for wealth as they have no coping mechanism for poverty. Thus, many Leos become wealthy. *Leos* enjoy quiet introspection and often choose hobbies where they spend time alone, interestingly, since they love the limelight.

Napoleon Bonaparte was born a *Leo* with a very strong personality. He had a short prominence as a French military leader during the Revolution.

King Henry V of England, also a *Leo*, was thought to be one of the strongest military leaders of the English Kings. Although he only served a nine-year reign, during the one hundred years of war.

Carl Gustav Jung, a *Leo* and psychologist, became best known for identifying the concept of collective unconsciousness. He apparently was very conscious when making this discovery.

Jerry Garcia, another *Leo*, is probably **grateful** to be **dead** because we are no longer *Dancing in the Streets*. He probably knocked on **heaven's door** just to get out of here.

Martha Stewart, a well-known model turned "Betty-home-maker" is best known for her cooking and decorating abilities and is also a *Leo*. She certainly knows how to make lemonade from lemons regardless of life's obstacles. She should be best known for her business successes.

Jackie Kennedy Onassis another well-known *Leo*, was best known for marrying men of power. She was the first lady to President John F. Kennedy and then married the world's richest and famous Greek shipping magnate, Aristotle Onassis.

Amelia Earhart was another famous *Leo*. Her career took flight as an aviation pioneer being the first female aviator to fly across the Atlantic Ocean. As an author, her books flew to popularity!

These are great examples of perseverance in war, business, power and recognition.

However, the biggest fear for the *Leo* rejection. Remember, the Lion believes he is top-cat! The *Leo's* next fear is restlessness and boredom. So, if he gets rejected, he'll quickly run! Intimacy follows as their third fear and then insecurity. Again, with the *Leo*, these run together. Is it jealousy that has one believe they need to be top cat? And, is it jealousy to believe that everyone is having more fun than you?

■  ■  ■

When born under the sign of **Virgo,** you have a feminine pull or polarity. Go figure, it is the symbol of the divine feminine virgin. *Virgo* is an earth sign. The *Virgo Sign* starts in late August and runs through the third week of September. *Virgos* love to use their academic, shrewd, practical, logical minds, especially to prove themselves correct and another incorrect. If you notice the sky looks blue, the *Virgo* will probably tell you it looks azure.

They possess great abilities with math and concentration, making wonderful accountants.

*Virgos* are modest, idealistic and analytical, however that tends to make them narrow-minded, critical and unimaginative. *Virgos* are often associated with the goddess-virgin woman symbols and think they should be treated as such ... even when not applicable.

Self-doubt appears to be the biggest enemy of the *Virgo*. If conquered there is no holding the *Virgo* back. Very versatile and surprisingly talented in many areas, the *Virgo* still can be quite delicate and requires security in life. Financial stability and a good job are necessary.

Relatively self-reliant, the *Virgo* often does well in the health-care field. *Virgos* can go from one extreme to the other, acting prudish to having a great fondness for the pleasure of the flesh. Both tendencies must be reconciled. Although ambitious in many areas, being mushy is not one, staying detached and cool. They may disregard the opinion of others if it differs from their own.

They love to keep busy, for without plenty to do their energy can become negative and critical of the entire world. Some *Virgos* feel best when having a link to the welfare of helping others. Part of that is their own ego, believing they know what is best for all.

Appearing as shy and meek, their inner qualities of determination and courage are often hidden. The *Virgo* considers themselves the ultimate professional which makes them tend to forget the personal side of others.

Worrying tends to make the *Virgo* a hypochondriac, blowing small symptoms out of proportion. Their digestive tract and skin are the areas of concern. Relaxation over worrying will help the symptoms.

*Virgoans* love to keep busy with many hobbies which could result in a business but for the disbelief in themselves. They love challenging situations and the ability to solve a problem.

Keen students are *Virgos*, loving the ability to add to their present achievements. If able to stay calm and physical, the *Virgo* will have tangible and lasting contentment. Often meditation is helpful to *Virgos*.

Confucius say, "I am a *Virgo* and I am known for my Chinese philosophy and politics regarding personal morality, governmental morality, correctness in social relationships, justice, kindness and sincerity." Confucius certainly had an opinion on morality.

Caligula, a Roman Emperor and also *Virgo* born, had no morality and was recorded as being a cruel and unpredictable leader putting many people to death. His reign was shaped by lunacy and lust.

Rachel Welch, a sex symbol and another *Virgo*, was made an icon in the 1960s and 1970s due to her portrayal as a strong female character, breaking the sex symbol mold. Her career was, indeed, one **fantastic voyage.**

Jesse Owens, born a *Virgo*, had controlled passion in the face of persecution. He was a dominant track-and-field athlete during the 1936 Olympics winning four gold medals despite being advised not to attend.

Agatha Christie, as a *Virgo* was no virgin to writing. She made herself famous through writing over seventy detective novels, certainly a sign of her steadfastness. Under the name of Mary Westmacott, she wrote six romance novels.

Mama Cass Elliot, *Virgo* born, **made her own kind of music** and excelled in her singing abilities to stardom only to die before her time; all the while writing and singing many love songs.

Dr. Joyce Brothers was best known not for being a *Virgo* but rather for her advice in counseling as a world-renowned psychologist and columnist. She was really known for her marriage and sex advice.

All of these *Virgos* are definitely not virgins, but all being consumed with passion, love and sex!

Insecurity is the number one fear of the *Virgo*! Unfortunately, rejection ranks number two in their fears; one fear feeding the other. Ironically, they fear intimacy which doesn't appear to go hand and hand with their interest in passion, love and sex. Lastly, *Virgos* fear boredom and restlessness in life. This sounds like jealousy ... fearing that everyone is better than you.

■　■　■

If born between the last week in September to the third week of October, you are born under the sign of **Libra.** A masculine polarity or pull, the *Libra* is an air sign.

More than anything, a *Libra* requires fairness and harmony wherever possible. Decisions are carefully considered before acting on any. They are born with love of beautiful things and spend their days making themselves happy while acquiring things.

The *Libra* is the sign of the scales thus having the need for justice. This includes their need to feel vindicated in their desires. They attempt to live up to their own ideals sometimes missing opportunities to make the right decision while wondering. They need the world to be balanced and anything upsetting the balance, in their mind, should be avoided.

They have charm and wit along with abundant social skills. They are people pleasers as it would not be tolerable for the *Libra* to not be liked by all. Projecting perfectionism is always the skill of the *Libra*.

*Libras* are likely to offer plenty of advice but lack the ability to practice what they preach. They love many friends and lots of conversation. *Libras* work best with others although are very capable of holding their own with their excellent mind. *Libras* do not like being alone and have the strong desire for a deep partnership. *Libras* crave all the comforts of home and find it difficult to do without.

Although *Libras* draw a strong line between personal and professional relationships, they can be very protective of close family and friends.

*Librans* are extremely image-conscious and concern themselves too much with wearing the right clothing. They can be obsessive about it to the degree of vanity and self-absorption.

It is difficult for a *Libran* to not partake in indulgent living, especially if not on their dollar. This eventually takes a toll, forcing the *Libra* to slow down and take better care. The kidneys and liver are the main areas of concern.

They can be emotional and have a soft heart but pride does not always lend itself to showing imperfection to others.

Mahatma Gandhi, born at the end of September, is best known for being a spiritual leader and pacifist, against Britain and for India. He apparently didn't have good foresight because although he is known for his quote: "An eye for an eye only ends up making the whole world blind," he did not see his own assassination coming.

Margaret Thatcher, an October *Libra*, gained her fame as the British prime minister nicknamed the Iron Lady. And iron she was. She once said, "Power is like being a lady. If you have to tell people you are, you aren't."

John Lennon born an October *Libran*, made himself known as the founder of the Beatles. Later, he was remembered as an activist for peace. **Imagine** if he still lived today, maybe we'd give **peace a chance.**

Ralph Lauren by design, was born a *Libra*. He may have been a little skittish about being Yiddish when he decided to design American clothes. He has, indeed, made his mark in the fashion world.

Dwight D. Eisenhower served as thirty-fourth president of the United States and also a *Libra*. He served as Chief General during WW II. However, in his unique *Libra* thinking, he weighed in with a famous quote, "Every gun that is made, every war ship launched, every rocket fired, signifies, in the final sense, a theft from those who hunger and are not fed and those who are cold and are not clothed."

Brigitte Bardot began as the beautiful blond actress of movies and later became an animal activist and the originator of the Brigitte Bardot Foundation dedicated to animal protection and rights.

Cheryl Tiegs, was well *suited* to being the first American supermodel. Both were *Libras.*

Julie Andrews, another October *Libra*, is well-known for her beautiful singing voice. We are certain the *Sound of Music, Mary Poppins and Victor Victoria* are **a few of her favorite things.**

The *Libra* has their greatest fear in intimacy and in others learning who they really are! So, being absorbed with appearing as the picture of perfection, their second fear falls into the arena of fearing rejection. Insecurity, I suppose, would force the *Libra* to look better than everyone else. And, being restless and bored in one's own life certainly falls into jealousy over someone else's life. The *Libra's* fears are tightly woven together.

■  ■  ■

**Scorpio** individuals are born under the pull or polarity of the feminine trait. It is another water sign and symbolized by the *Scorpion.* The sign starts in the third week of October and ends in the third week of November.

*Scorpios* require 100 percent commitment from others and are jealous by their very nature. They consider themselves to be both potent and passionate. *Scorpios* can be creatively imaginative. However, sometimes their creative imagination also creates an inflated self-worth.

As the *Scorpio* expects 100 percent from everyone, they easily remember when anyone gives less than that amount and remember it until they are dead and buried. Forgiveness is not their forte.

Insufficient exercise leaves the *Scorpio* feeling out of sorts and out of balance.

They are powerful yet temperamental leaders with the ability to lead a revolt when necessary. Often that ability is not necessary and lends itself to *unnecessary* destruction.

*Scorpios* love sharing their intense emotions in a relationship, finding it mandatory. They often appear to evolve several times throughout their life, gaining wisdom and completeness as they transform.

They can have the tendency to become single-minded and must be careful to apply balance to everything in life. Otherwise, either work or family will become neglected. They take full responsibility for their actions but in a cavalier manner, answering to no one.

Balance is of the utmost importance to the *Scorpio*. Having many passions and talents, deciding what to focus on seems to be difficult for them. Once goals are set, however, they achieve to meet their success. *Scorpios* must take time to relax or they will burn themselves out. They are self-starters with a high level of ambition.

It's important for *Scorpios* to be private, keeping their personal lives to themselves. They have a need for self-preservation. They attempt at all costs to look powerful, often placing themselves in a position where their guard cannot be let down. Then, they risk social and emotional isolation.

*Scorpios* possess a strong desire for wealth and are very jealous of others, forgetting to find thankfulness in their own gifts.

Ted Turner, a well-known *Scorpio*, apparently is dynamite as in TNT, at networking. He is best known as a media proprietor, producer and philanthropist. He founded the Cable News Network, the first twenty-four-hour news channel.

Robert Kennedy, also a *Scorpio* born in November, served the United States as the sixty-fourth attorney general and was a presidential candidate after his brother John, before his own assassination. He apparently had a lot of **seconds,** to his brother John.

Bo Derek, born a *Scorpio*, gained her fame in the movie *10*, a sex comedy. Ten was probably the number of braids she wore on her head.

Marie Antoinette was born as a *Scorpio*. Although she may appear to have liked cake, she actually never said, "Let them eat cake." It appeared that she lost her mind, when it actually was her head.

Georgia O'Keeffe is best known as the Mother of American Modernism in painting, including many flowers. She said, "I hate flowers. I only paint them because they are cheaper than models and they don't move." She was an American artist born under the *Sign* of *Scorpio*.

Charles Manson was born in November and famously known as an American criminal and cult leader. He coerced his followers into committing nine murders. So, I guess a *Scorpio* can be deadly!

Martin Luther is well-known for leading the Protestant Reformation against the Catholic church as a priest and *Scorpio*, creating the Lutheran Church. Scorpios love to shake things up. Maybe he reformed, as a Lutheran.

The fear of the *Scorpio* is ironic. They fear above and beyond anything else, betrayal. Yet, they are the first to betray. I guess we fear what we are most guilty of. Fearing they will self-destruct is their second biggest fear, because the *Scorpio* is concerned with their own poisonous self. Their third and fourth greatest fears are loss and failure which go hand and hand for the *Scorpio*. Their failure would be a personal loss ... since they don't believe they can fail.

If born under **Sagittarius** your birthday is between the middle of November to the middle of December. It is also a fire sign and has masculine polarity or pull. *Sagittarians* are represented by the Archer or Centaur, which is half man, half horse. What does this mean? The *Sagittarian* will either shoot you, verbally or physically, or, be compassionate and can work like a horse. Both restless and emotionally warm, the *Sagittarian* often finds conventional life to be rather restrictive. And, they will rebel when feeling oppressed.

Their impulsive enthusiasm and impatience can tend to hinder a focused approach. Therefore, as parents, *Sagittarians* tend to be a bit too preachy and push their beliefs onto their children. Their opinions are quite firm with an uncompromising directness. So strong is their opinion, they are often looked upon as interfering.

They have a bold and optimistic attitude, positive outlook and adventurous spirit. There is an expansive desire for discovery and new challenges. Their focus on professional and intellectual goals makes them somewhat single-minded. The emotional needs of others as well as their own tend to be neglected.

Loving to travel abroad with an interest in other countries, goes hand and hand with their spirit, longing to be free. When becoming too stagnate, the *Sagittarian* will search for an escape.

*Sagittarians* possess a great sense of humor and enjoy sharing humor with others. They also have exceptional organization and practical skills.

It is extremely important for the *Sagittarian* to remember to take a break from work and business. Otherwise, they will continue to plow on and eventually burn out completely.

The strong and independent nature of the *Sagittarian* allows them to quickly learn what trouble is and avoid it. *Sagittarians* need a self-assured partner who makes them feel loved as well as free. And, their active and physical lifestyle will help to keep them healthy and alive.

Tina Turner, best known for her rocking-out ability, rolled right down the river as a *Sagittarian*. Another well-known *Sagittarian*, not just a **little woman**, was Louisa May Alcott who wrote about her belief in strong, independent women. In her books, there were no **little women** but rather little minds. Another famous singer and *Sagittarian* is Bette Midler, singing as if the **wind was beneath her wings.**

Samuel Langhorne Clemens, better known as Mark Twain, was born a *Sagittarian*, writing with great imagination in *The Adventures of Huckleberry Finn* and *Tom Sawyer*; two very determined characters, determined to impress Becky Thatcher.

He's maybe not the most talented but the most tenacious of golfers, Lee Trevino, was also born under the sign of *Sagittarius*. He was confident in his ability to make any shot and then admitting it was, as he meant it to be.

And, speaking of guns and determination, George Armstrong Custer took a stand until it killed him. Henry VI, famous for being a bit *loco en la cabeza*, or otherwise known as a bit crazy, was ruling as he pleased and not as was expected. He was prolific with starting universities but too scattered to lead an army. These individuals exhibited rather typical *Sagittarian* qualities of determination and of mental escape.

An overwhelming first fear of the *Sagittarian* is of failure. Because, the Sag. truly does not believe they can fail. Secondly, betrayal would look like they had failed. The *Sagittarian* often feels as if everyone around them is a betrayal! Fear of self-destruction is third in their list of fears and lastly fear of loss. The *Sagittarian* believes loss is somehow related to losing; therefore, they make sure it doesn't happen. Forgiving others is never on their bucket list, because *Sagittarians* do not make mistakes.

■ ■ ■

And, at long last ... **Capricorn**-born people have a feminine polarity or pull, beginning in the third week of December through the third week of January. They are an earth sign. The sign of *Capricorn* is the horned goat. What does that mean? It means that *Capricorns* are both ambitious and reliable yet tend toward climbing the mountain, requiring material security.

Those born under this sign are ambitious and place great value on achieving their goals. They are careful planners about their future and cling to it with tenacity. However, they remain pessimistic in their thinking. They require organization and to have their life well-thought out. They unfortunately place greater value on achieving career aims than on nurturing their relationships.

A *Capricorn* is responsible with very high moral standards and is rather traditional, sticking to their tried-and-true methods. *Capricorns* have a need for a family and security.

They are slightly pushy toward their own needs which sometimes causes others to respond in opposition. A *Capricorn* expects their children to perform highly and is disappointed in those who do not, making that child feel unsuccessful.

A *Capricorn* may appear arrogant and unwilling to listen to any advice or criticism no matter how productive.

A warm and reserved personality, the *Capricorn* tends to mellow with age. Although they have a domineering tendency throughout life. The *Capricorn* appears to have an ingrained sense of obligation and duty but should remain careful not to miss out on potential happiness by taking on unnecessary obligation.

Those born under the sign of *Capricorn* are deeply motivated to obtain security in life. They are frugal with money and uncomfortable spending their money on what they believe to be frivolous things. They like to work hard at their jobs which can cause stress-related problems.

Sir Isaac Newton, a well-known scientist was born a *Capricorn*. He was a **force** to be reckoned with. You can't really **monkey** around with this particular *Capricorn* and famous teen idol, Davey Jones.

Paul Revere was born as a *Capricorn* and famous as a patriot during the American Revolution. One if by land, two if by sea and I on the opposite shore will be. Pushy *Capricorn*.

Sew, this next famous woman was also born under the *Capricorn* S*ign* and as Betsy Ross she was responsible for the stars and stripes that would last forever. Keeping with inventing, Benjamin Franklin was also born under the horned goat *Sign* of *Capricorn*. Oh Benjamin, "Go fly a kite!"

Jean Dixon was a well-known American psychic. Wonder if she predicted she'd be born as a *Capricorn*? Alexander Hamilton was the first secretary of the treasury under George Washington. Obviously, he was born as a *Capricorn* with his money management skills, spending other people's money. These are great examples of those born under the *Capricorn* sign.

To the *Capricorn*, fearing loss of any kind is devasting to their psyche. Failure to them is fear of loss as well! It's a competition. The *Capricorn's* fear of loss extends into and through their fear of self-destruction. Lacking self-care always results in self-destruction … knowing this and still not taking care, is truly a loss! Betrayal is usually of themselves and their needs, still they fear it! But, forgiving others who they deem betrayed them, is necessary but doesn't happen with the *Capricorn*. Unforgiveness begins within themselves with failure, loss, care and since this sign is negligent in their own care and forgiveness, how will they forgive others?

■   ■   ■

Those born at the end of the astrological sign or the first day of an astrological sign tend to exhibit traits from both astrological signs. For example, an *Aquarian* born on the eighteenth of February would naturally pull *Piscean* tendencies as the next day, February nineteenth, would be under that sign. One usually takes on more of the traits of the upcoming sign as a cusp-born person. But that is not always the definitive.

■　■　■

*Elizabeth Speaks ...*

It's about love. It has always been about love. It is about overcoming the obstacles that we ourselves have created to love.

With Henry and Sussan, the obstacles seemed great. However, consider the *Astrological Signs* to be gifts to help them overcome. They were never alone; Angels and Spirit Guides were there to help them. They were placed together again for strength to overcome. Despite the world they lived in full of war, deceit, power and conceit, God gave them help to overcome.

They had lessons and fears to conquer. God gave them each other to hold onto. Call it a spark of love. The original spark of love; a spark that really has no beginning and no end.

Then, consider Henry and Sussan's next life as Giovanni and Katrina. What Giovanni first noticed was a spark or fire in Katrina's eyes. Specific Signs with specific Angels were meant to help them heal and cause their relationship to grow.

Consider Sussan's journey. She was a woman who had everything taken from her. She had no choice in her relationship. She was owned, abused, raped and beaten until Henry. Then, as Katrina, she was given every material object thus, when given Giovanni, she did not see she had received love which is everything. She did, however, learn to overcome her **Libra** tendencies and appreciate love more than material things.

Then, consider their next lives as Robert and Sarah. It was in England in the 1600s. During that life there was no obstacle not easily overcome. There was *Ahav* and *Ahava*, even in death.

*To be continued ...*

## Chapter 8

# Elements and the Elementals

Now that we understand how we were created and that there is a specific framework that God places us in with each reincarnation, we should understand that we actually helped to create our own framework through our choices after our initial incarnation that is. God, then, modified our astrological signs, traits and archetypes. God modified it through what we refer to as *Elementals* or modifiers. Remember, the astrological signs are also classified under elements.

The *elements:*

1. Air

2. Fire

3. Water

4. Earth

Air- Aquarius, Libra and Gemini

Fire – Aries, Leo and Sagittarius

Water – Pisces, Cancer and Scorpio

Earth – Capricorn, Taurus and Virgo

*And*

The *Elementals:*

1. Air

2. Fire

3. Water

4. Earth

Many of you have heard these elements or descriptors in correlation with astrological signs. These are related but not the same as described in horoscope books. The elements as explained in the horoscope books are not simply attached to a sign. In addition to these elements, there are other *Elementals* attached by God and decided by God as modifiers to assist with tendencies in our personality, meant to aid them on our paths. These *Elementals* are:

*Air – Life force and breath. Head-thinker, knowledge or curiosity.*

*Fire – Passion, inspiration. Energy or impulsive.*

*Water – Muted or calming. Flowing or emotional.*

*Earth – Grounded, nurturing. Practical or deliberate.*

God attaches only two *Elementals*. They could be attached to the astrology sign, the trait or the archetype. It is possible that our zodiac sign will not get an *Elemental*. It is God's choice. These *Elementals* can be applied in various methods from one on a sign, to two on a sign or one on a trait or two on a trait, or two on an archetype, or one on archetype. But there are only two *Elementals* per soul.

What is the purpose of the *Elementals?* We understand, as explained in more detail in a later chapter, that our only choice, directly, is in our archetype. If we choose not to take the advice of our Spirit Guide and make a poor choice, God may choose to modify the Archetype with *Water*, for example, which *Waters* down that choice.

Another example of using an *Elemental* as in *Fire* would be to insight passion. Let's say we chose a Lover archetype under the advice of our Spirit Guide. God may choose to modify that for the good, with *Fire* for more passion and more desire to connect. Or God could be disappointed in our choice and attach *Water* to the Lover archetype and lessen the passion or connection.

Using the *Elemental* of *Earth* on a Loon trait will reinforce the Loon's choice to stay in the nest and not take flight. The *Earth Elemental* will ground the Loon and make them more nurturing. But, applying a *Fire Elemental* to the Loon could encourage them to make decisions impulsively and possibly fly the coop.

Let's say you're a Capricorn astrological sign. Capricorns are careful planners. Applying the *Air Elemental* to this sign could cause a near paralysis on planning, being stuck in their head forever. Applying a *Water Elemental* could *Water* down or mute their plan or make them more emotional which is often needed.

Suppose two "Intended" Lover archetypes are placed in a reincarnation. Unless there is a very specific karmic debt, God would not apply two *Fires* to each archetype on both individuals.

Having that much passion between the two Lovers could potentially burn out. *Water* would most likely be attached to one of them to cool down and calm the *Fire*. In a truly connected Lover/Lover relationship the *Fire* is shared and the *Water* is shared, bringing an even more emotional bond.

**AIR – The Air Elemental/modifier is about breath or life force.** However, it could also be about the head, *Air*-head or not. It can also mean thinker, knowledge or curiosity. The *Air*-head tends to have a negative connotation to it and the thinker, knowledge, curiosity aspect, does not. For good reason. However, the *Air*-head we would assume does not think about anything but it could mean that the *Air*-head does not take themselves too seriously. That is the positive aspect to the *Air*-head along with being nonjudgmental. *Air* is a life force. It feeds *Fire*. It moves *Water* and can even cause some waves. However, it only affects the surface of the *Earth*.

**FIRE – The Fire Elemental/modifier is about adding fuel to the Fire or lighting of the Fire.** Consider it a nudge to a passive personality. Being easy-going is certainly considered a positive trait. However, that is much different than thinking there is no hurry in making a decision. Adding a *Fire Elemental* to a slow decision maker will hopefully speed things along. *Fire* will add some strength and accountability. *Fire* will also inspire and energize the passive personality or otherwise. We all understand how passion effects a relationship. *Fire* will ignite the passion. *Air* feeds the *Fire*, *Earth* can smother the *Fire* but it will still smolder and, literally, only *Water* can cool the *Fire*.

**WATER – The Water Elemental/modifier calms all other modifiers and signs.** If you can imagine, *Water* puts out the *Fire*. *Water* feeds the *Earth*. If splashed in their face, *Water* can wake up the *Air* sign. However, adding *Water* to *Water* just makes a bigger puddle. *Water* is also cleansing or purifying and can soothe a soul or sign. *Water* is also nourishing and second only to *Air* as a requirement of life force. However, combining *Air* and *Water* causes a storm. That storm can be positive or negative depending on the trait, astrological sign or archetype. *Fire* cannot shake the *Earth* but *Water* can wear the *Earth* down. And, when *Air* and *Water* are mixed, they can literally reform the *Earth* with that storm.

**EARTH – The Earth Elemental/modifier grounds all other modifiers and signs.** It is steadfast and least likely to be affected by the other modifiers. It can be resistant to change which is why *Water* can eventually wear it down because of the slow process. Therefore, the *Earth Elemental* can be molded but not transformed. *Earth* is very nurturing and the source of all other nutrition. *Fire* can only char the surface unless *Fire* is applied deeply and, in that case, it may cause the volcano to erupt. *Air* and *Water* applied together can mold the *Earth* more quickly. The *Earth* modifier can strengthen the tendencies of any astrological sign or archetype; or make them more nurturing.

## Chapter 9

# Elementals/Modifiers on the Signs

## *Aquarius*

When you think of the Aquarius sign, you picture a water-bearer. But they are, in fact, an air sign. The Aquarian certainly has curiosity and an intellectual side. If an *Air* modifier is applied to an Aquarian, it accentuates the curiosity. Too much *Air* applied to the Aquarian makes them an *Air*-head.

Aquarians already have a strong sense of what is right. However, applying the *Air Elemental* could make them ever so stubborn in their approach. They will be determined in insisting what they believe is correct.

Applying the *Fire* modifier to the Aquarian can literally make them breathe *Fire*. It can also make them more passionate about their curiosity. In fact, it can make them more passionate about everything. For the Aquarian, who can be in their head as an air sign, it can draw them out of their head and into their heart which is where their passion really lives.

Adding the *Water* modifier to the Aquarian air sign can mute or calm the sign. However, if excited, it can now create a force of nature. *Water* is soothing; *Water* and air can produce beautiful, relaxing waves or a Tsunami.

Adding the *Earth* modifier to the Aquarian air sign can, of course, strengthen the Aquarian qualities. And, it can also make them more nurturing.

Two modifiers can be applied to either the astrological sign, the trait, or the archetype, remember.

Here is an example of applying two modifiers to the Aquarian sign: If *Water* is applied to the Aquarian there is the potential for a storm. Then applying *Earth* as a modifier, the potential for a storm lessens. So, God may be intent on causing a force of nature, yet decreases the volatility effect with the *Earth* modifier. It is all based on karma and the effect required.

### Pisces

Pisces is a water sign. Why would God apply an *Air Elemental* to this water sign? The nature of the Piscean is already to ask themselves which way to swim. Adding the *Air Elemental* further places them in indecisiveness and further into the head. However, it can make the Piscean move closer to being a force of nature.

Adding the *Fire* modifier to a Pisces may light a *Fire* under their behind! It can also make them less indecisive and transform the soft, loving nature into a blaze of passion. In fact, it can make their water boil!

A *Water* modifier applied to the water sign can reinforce the calming nature of this sign. But too much *Water* can just create a sink hole.

Another example of applying two modifiers, would be *Fire* and *Water*. In that case, all that *Fire* and *Water* produces steam.

*Earth*-modifying Pisces can strengthen the Piscean character and make them less wishy-washy. If you applied *Earth* and *Water* to Piscean or any sign you would make them an easy-going nurturer.

Of course, applying *Earth* anytime to Pisces can make them even more grounded. But adding too much *Earth* to Pisces just makes muddy water.

## Aries

Aries falls under the fire sign. Putting an *Air Elemental* on a fire sign is feeding the fire. Arians already possess volatile temperaments. Adding *Air* to the Aries can make them more easily angered. It can also make them go further in their own head and create stubbornness and even more determined to be know-it-alls. There is not much worse a personality than a know-it-all *Air*-head.

*Fire* with the Aries causes passion with those things they like to do. They can be romantically passionate, however, with the Aries, too much *Fire* makes them burn out. The *Fire* modifier can also make them successful at work IF they like what they do. And, liking what they do is their passion. If it ain't fun and I'm an Aries, I ain't doing it.

The *Water* modifier applied to the Aries will slightly calm the Aries, however, just like the horse, sometimes you can lead them to *Water* but they will not drink. But, applying *Water* to Aries will make it easier for them to go with the flow. Although *Water* is normally muting, don't expect it to shut the Aries up. And, finally, if you applied *Water* and *Water Elementals* to the Aries, you will put out their fire and they will accomplish nothing.

Adding the *Earth* modifier to the Arian does bring out the nurturing quality. However, it may make the Aries even more stubborn and hard to move. And, applying *Earth* to an Arian may only feed their ego. The Arian already gets lost in their thoughts of strength, ego and capabilities. So, in conclusion, after reading all of the above, you will find that modifying the Aries sign is hardly worth the effort. God would be much more satisfied modifying the trait or archetype.

## Taurus

Taureans fall under the earth sign. They can be rather depend-able and strong, yet stubborn. Although they are an earth sign, they sometimes lack nurturing. Applying an *Air* modify to this earth sign barely moves the surface. It basically raises a little dust and sometimes the Taurean will just sweep it back under the carpet.

Adding *Fire* to this earth sign may scorch the surface but it will not change their basic nature unless the *Fire* gets deep within them; and then, they may explode. Adding the *Fire* to the Taurus sign will increase their passion at least on the surface.

*Water* as a modifier to the Taurus sign has the greatest chance to change them. *Water* can slowly wear down and calm the Taurus. Because it can slowly change it, it can make the edges of the earth Taurus less sharp. But, adding *Water* to the earth twice will simply flood it and cause it to be totally washed out.

*Earth* modifying on the earth sign at first sounds counter-productive making them immoveable. However, the *Earth* modi-fier to an earth sign actually makes them a much better nurturer.

## Gemini

Another air sign, the twin-Geminis have an outgoing, fun-loving part to their character. However, applying an *Air Elemental* to this could work to the better adding to that nature. But, apply-ing the *Air Elemental* when the Gemini is in their negative frame, will only add to their less thoughtful state. So, probably adding an *Air Elemental* to this sign should be carefully pondered with karma-related issues. God would not want to add an *Air Elemental* to an already two-faced nature. Remember, it is God who will be making these decisions, not us.

*Fire Elemental*, on the Gemini air sign, again must have you consider both sides of the twins. It can make them fun-loving, passionate lovers or the air may be so hot that you are scorched.

In the Gemini when applying *Fire*, it may also be wise to apply *Water*. After all, there are two sides here in the twins. God could ignite their passion and calm their poison adding these modifiers. In fact, applying *Water* to the Gemini may calm their overall business-only sense; creating a little more softness and a little more humanitarian traits. Dare we say a bit more compassionate? NO!

Adding the *Earth Elemental* to the Gemini will definitely create a more nurturing and grounded twin. They may even stay home two or three days a week. If God would apply *Earth* and *Earth Elementals* to the Gemini sign with a wonderful partner, you could almost make them great parents. Applying the *Earth* and keeping them more grounded makes it much easier for the Gemini to stay on the fun-loving side of the twins.

## Cancer

Those born under Cancer are also water signs. Cancers are typically loyal family members, relatively direct by nature, hard-working but self-saboteurs with very addictive behavior. Applying the *Air* modifier to a Cancer sign can potentially cause them to live further into their own heads. However, this could be a plus. Perhaps, the Cancer would think before using their very sharp tongue. It may make the Cancer question whether they need one more drink; therefore God would probably not modify them with two *Airs* causing them to wish to escape even their own thoughts ... which could push them to that next drink. (Unless karma warrants it).

Therefore, two *Airs* mixed with this water sign could lead to a storm that cannot be escaped. Consider a soul who was considerably controlling in a past life. God may choose to add the two *Air* modifiers causing this soul to be controlled by alcohol in this life. In this case, the only way the self-saboteur can get through this life is with love of self and others ... and isn't that always the point?

*Fire* and the Cancer. Spontaneous combustion! *Fire* applied to this sign will most certainly add heat to the sharp, hot dagger tongue. It will also make their water-nature boil. The positive side to adding the *Fire Elemental* to this sign is the passion added to their family loyalty; and, a little heat to their cool, aloof nature. Allowing the Cancer to boil over in that water sign gives them an outlet to not hold so much in; holding in causes further addictive behavior.

Adding or modifying with additional *Water* to the Cancer water sign blunts the sharp tongue, calms the addictive behavior and can overall cause them to go with the flow. *Water* soothes, dilutes, neutralizes and nourishes. However, too much *Water*, by modifying with two *Water Elementals* can take their already sentimental nature and make the *Water* flow with tears.

There is a difference between loyalty to family and nurturing. Adding the *Earth* modifier to the Cancer sign can truly transform from loyal to loving. There is a difference from protecting them and keeping them as they are and nurturing, letting them be who they should be. For example, being there for your children is admirable but if you are only there to nurture when it suits your needs is much different than being there while they grow possibly in another direction than yours. After all, you could grow toward them in their adulthood. We are always learning and growing. There is comfort in keeping things exactly the same; however, there is no growth should things and life remain exactly the same. *Earth* stabilizes and grounds the Cancer, thus also decreases their addictive behavior.

## Leo

The lion falls under the fire sign. I am the king of you and I am the king of me. Adding an *Air Elemental* to Leo can make the fire smolder for long periods. They are seldom expressive, however, if that fire smolders for a very long time, they will enflame! *Air* can make the Leo contemplative ... however, that contemplation almost always leads to the conclusion that they are right!

*Fire* will make them a passionate leader; however, if no one follows they can burn with rage. *Fire* can also produce a passionate lover but they must lead the way! Never under any circumstances should a Leo be modified with two *Fires;* in this case, they become a dictator (again, unless karma insists).

And, we should remember that very few cats like to swim. So, adding *Water* to the Leo goes against their nature. But, if you add enough *Water* to fire, you can put them out. This cat will still try to swim upstream! So, it's probably not the best *Elemental* to choose.

One would think *Earth* can ground anything. In fact, *Earth* will keep a Leo home; otherwise, the Leo will be out searching for the next kill. Sometimes, the only slowing down of a Leo is to kick a little dirt or *Earth* in his face.

## Virgo

A Virgo is very much a feminine sign; that of the virgin or the maiden. The Virgo female is convinced in believing she is very much the divine female because of this. The male Virgo doesn't believe he has any feminine qualities ... he does not equate his emotions, his tenderness, or his sensitivity with his feminine side actually considering those as weaknesses. Another earth sign, of course, the Virgo needs to be an earth sign. They must be grounded! They already think too highly of themselves.

Why modify a Virgo with *Air?* You just shouldn't! *Air* will only touch the surface of the earth. You could try to modify the Virgo with two *Airs;* more *Air* causing their mind to move the thoughts off of their own.

Modifying the earth Virgo with *Fire* does bring out their passion. In fact, it can ignite and melt the ice caps on either pole; so, this could be a great choice to modify the Virgo with *Fire* and

*Water*. Modifying just with *Water* could cause a frozen Virgo and we don't need to add to their cold demeanor.

Modifying Virgo with *Water* has the most trickle-down effect. *Water* can mold this earth sign. Because *Water* can soften earth, it may bring out their true feminine or nurturing side.

*Earth* on earth? Excellent, as the Virgo does need to be grounded. It will also help them embrace motherhood or fatherhood.

## Libra

Libras as air signs are materialistic in their heads, their life force and with every breath they take; it is about appearance. If you are applying *Air* to Libra it is counterproductive and could cause them to be more materialistic and stuck on appearances.

Libra is also the sign of the scales. They are always weighing the value. If you apply an *Air* modifier, literally being too much in their head, they will have difficulty making a decision.

Adding a *Fire Elemental* to the Libra air sign does make them passionate about what is just and right! It will not make them less concerned with their appearance and appearing right, but it will make them passionate about other worldly concerns. Especially, if they are also modified with *Earth* as well, bringing them passion and grounding.

*Water* will calm the Libra. If they are too concerned with their appearance, they will weigh the facts and realize they are just all wet! This Libra will learn it is difficult to keep your hair perfect in the rain. *Water* applied to this sign leads to a gentle reign.

Modifying the air sign with an *Earth Elemental* creates more stability. They will better understand the weight of their decisions. *Earth* will additionally add to their nurturing capabilities.

## Scorpio

A water sign, like the arachnoid scorpion, lies a hard, outer shell. They try to protect themselves above and beyond everything else.

In general, the Scorpio possesses a calm and confident demeanor; however, their hard exterior is to protect them from their own insecurities. They trust no one but themselves and are willing to strike out and kill anyone breaking their trust.

They scurry from place to place keeping themselves busy; however, they are waiting to find their next prey. So, modifying with the *Air Elemental* just makes them consider themselves a bit smarter, remaining in their heads and making them more insecure. They may believe themselves to have more vital force, making them a force to be reckoned with … in the negative way.

*Fire* added to the Scorpio will make them more passionate; however, the relationships will be short-lived because the said Scorpio will sting and kill its mate! A Scorpio is always better with another Scorpio with each in possession of their hard, outer shell. Each will understand the other's jealous and distrustful nature; therefore, the way to soften the Scorpio is to modify with more *Water! Water* comforts, cools and calms the Scorpio. Adding both *Fire* and *Water* as modifiers makes them passionate and less likely to sting or kill you.

It's interesting, *Earth* never muddies the water of a Scorpio. However, it does make them better nurturers. Scorpios grow quite comfortable when modified by *Earth*.

## Sagittarius

A fire sign, it represents the centurion which is half man and half beast. With a Sag, you must know which one you are dealing with. They consider themselves either a hero or a warrior. One thinks with its head and one thinks by instinct alone. One aspect of the Sag can have a conversation and the other half can only fight or run. Thus, adding *Air* as a modifier can transform them into a dragon, who breathes more fire.

As a dragon, the sweep of their tail clears even a larger path for their fire. Sometimes, that means when they speak, it's nothing more than hot *Air*. Adding *Fire* to the Sag just feeds their ego, both hero and warrior; they literally do believe they are hot!

Modifying them with *Water* does cool the beast. Understand though, that if they walk through *Water*, it's only the beast below the surface. And, you can't add any more *Water*, like with two modifiers, for example, because in this case, the centurion will simply drown, putting out all of their fire.

*Earth*, when added to the Sag, will certainly create a more nurturing man/beast. It provides a stability, definitely needed by this sign. *Earth* does make the beast slightly stronger; and will remove them slightly from their own head and thinking, pulling their nature down.

## Capricorn

The horned-goat is also an earth sign. What does this mean? Remember with any horned-goat, there will be a butting of the heads, holding their ground. Capricorns tend to believe they and only they are right … if modified with an *Air Elemental* it further allows them in their own head, confirming they are right! If you make them an *Air*-head, they cannot even explain why they are right. Besides, *Air* again can do very little to change the surface of this earth sign.

Capricorns already believe they are alone in any work being completed. Lighting a *Fire* under them is useless. *Fire* could possibly motivate the Capricorn, but just how motivated should you make a horned animal on *Fire*? When adding *Fire* to the central core of the Capricorn you will just create lava which will flow and burn everything within its path.

*Water* added to the horned-goat, in this case, will enhance the nurturer, making their milk flow. Adding too much *Water* or two *Water* modifiers will keep the horned-goat stuck in the mud. *Water* does also soften the old goat!

*Earth* on earth. What does that accomplish? It definitely provides further nurturing from the Capricorn, especially when added with *Water.* In this case, the Capricorn has something to give.

*Elementals are just another form of etiquette ...*

Josephine was born a **Sagittarian** in Roxbury, Massachusetts, to wealthy, civic-minded parents in 1843. God had modified her sign with **water.** Being a strong **Sagittarian** woman helped her further her life; however, it did not further her compassion for others, a typical **Sag.** tendency.

After the early death of her brother during the Civil War, his widow, Annie became severely depressed. This began Josephine's interest in the mental health of her sister-in-law and all women. It might have been referred to as Melancholia in those days. In all reality, Josephine, too, suffered from Melancholia at the death of her favorite brother followed by the death of her husband the next year. She traveled abroad in the attempt to sooth her mourning.

Once returning from abroad, she took on the plight of mental health for women and women who were incarcerated in prison. She found a common thread between the women of both asylums and prisons to be sexual and other forms of abuse. Josephine, upon this discovery, assumed these women had weakness within them rather than finding the weakness in their perpetrators. Josephine had been born into wealth and comfort. She had not taken into consideration the differences between her lifestyle and upbringing versus the women inhabiting those institutions.

In her next life as Carla's mother, she was without the knowledge of hardship during the Depression. She continued to have dolls, fur coats and ample food. Although, she would, indeed, find financial hardship once married.

However, the fur coats and toys were a means of compensating for the sexual abuse at the hand of her father throughout her entire life, beginning before she was old enough to recall.

Realize, that as Josephine, she had the loss of her brother and husband and now in her next life, she had the loss of trust in her father.

Cindy, (Carla's mother), was born under the divine feminine sign of **Virgo** on the cusp. She believed herself to possess a certain sex appeal. The relationship with her husband was stimulating from a sexual standpoint but it could not replace any of the loss she carried over from her previous life. The **Virgo** fears most, insecurity and rejection. She had naturally carried insecurity due to the continued sexual abuse by her father and then, the insecurity and rejection roared its ugly head when her husband began to see another woman. Additionally, God modified her **Virgo** with **Earth** to ground her into nurturing.

Staying in their relationship appeared to be due to her Catholic upbringing; however, the fear of the **Virgo** also played a large part in her continuing in a relationship that she could not find security and stability in.

God had modified Cindy's Virgo with the elemental of **Earth** to ground her, knowing a rejection in this relationship might send her looking for her own comfort and it enabled her to be a better nurturer of her daughters. She had been given a green Angel of jealousy to help her rid feelings she harbored toward those with better relationships.

This, of course, was due to a tendency that began with Josephine who was jealous of those who still had a husband after the war.

One of the lessons of this life as Cindy was that she was not to be defined by the type of male attention she received. She had lack of attention as Josephine. However, as Cindy, she received male attention, but in a nefarious manner. Cindy had to learn to not let the abuse of her father and neglect of her husband affect who she was. Unfortunately, she stayed in the relationship with her children's father much too long and to the point of a near nervous breakdown. When she did finally leave him, she did not take her daughters along until she remarried a couple of years later.

This ties into the karma of Ms. Orsini, Katrina's mother. Cindy remarried the same man who was formerly known as the Cardinal Alessandro Farnese, Katrina's father, to provide as he had to Ms. Orsini previously. She had stayed once to provide for her daughter and then again in another life, this one, to provide for her daughters.

Cindy was still victimized in her new marriage; just as the women of the prisons and the asylums had been in her previous life as Josephine. Cindy learned compassion for all the people around her and even in her abusive husband in her dying days.

Cindy's final lesson in this life was when she could no longer care for herself, her children were there to care for her.

In her end days, she learned to laugh at her disease. Sharing the laughter with her children was more important than angering at the state she was now in. It was not the brain tumor or the man she was married to that would define her final days as unhappy.

Remember Ms. Orsini … now Cindy, was trying to teach Katrina (Carla) who suffered with polio, one last lesson. It's not the disease that defines you or, in her own case, the man you are now married to. It's not what happens to you but rather how you choose to react.

Cindy thought she heard music. She stood in a long, flowing gown. A handsome, young man in a Civil War uniform asked her for one last dance. It was none other than her husband as Josephine. She swirled around the dance floor, skirt swinging and her feet never touching the ground. She could see all of the lights flickering around her and felt dizzy. She was becoming disassociated with her senses.

Her last thought, because she could not say, "Stop!" was, "What about my girls?" She felt as if she was cradled in Angel wings and was safe and warm. Then, she heard Carla's grandfather (Carla's father's father) say, "I want you to remember your last thought."

She went through her past-life review with one of her daughters at her side. Her daughter, who had preceded her in death, had passed her over from Earth to the spiritual world. It was the first time that Patrice had taken a soul from this physical world to Atonement. Patrice was assisted by a young, dark-skinned girl with small hands.

Cindy was in Atonement for seven years. In 2003, God offered Cindy a role where she could remain in the spiritual world and continue to learn lessons. She would learn to nurture the passed-over animals of her soul-family and watch over her children, keeping negative energy from them. Then, in 2015, God so eloquently announced to Cindy that she had completed her lessons and could go Over the Horizon where souls go who no longer reincarnate.

Cindy's response to God was, "But, how can I leave my children when they need me most?" God responded, "But Cindy, isn't that what this was all about?" God knew she would choose her children and be selfless, this time.

*You're welcome ...*
*Isabella.*

## Chapter 10

# Traits ... Written in Nature

We are back to seeing twelve once again in the number of possible *Traits* we could have attached to us. *Traits* are assigned with each reincarnation by God. Our *Trait* is not our decision as is the case with our astrological sign. God chooses our *Trait* to assist us on our path and to ensure growth and evolution with each reincarnation. Sometimes they remain the same in each life but often they change. And, sometimes they gradually change to another *Trait* during a lifetime because of our actions.

**WARM – In the beginning everyone had the Warm Trait and could hear GOD speaking to them.** You may remember reading in the Old Testament of the Bible how God spoke with Adam, Noah, Abraham, Hagar and many more. Over time, people ignored God and allowed other traits to take over decreasing their ability to hear God.

*Warm* is the first sensation you experience at birth. It manifests as comfort and it's usually with a parent. The feeling which is *Warm* and like a loving parent is God.

All other *Traits* are related to karma. Children gain karmic debt *Traits* through their parents' karma, if the parents do not break the cycle.

Our other *Traits* come about because of our poor choices on purpose, either during a lifetime or after that lifetime.

*Warm Trait* persons are more open-minded and open in general. They have the ability to hear the spiritual world.

Unfortunately, though, they tend to be more idealistic which can cause naiveté. Purity of heart is always good but can make the *Warm* person unaware of another's intentions or motives. There often is no filter in their thinking making their projection of the truth innocent and not vindictive. Innocence and naiveté does leave a person open to being hurt. Thus, forgiveness is a goal for the *Warm Trait* person. Otherwise, that *Warm Trait* can morph into another karmic *Trait*.

Unforgiveness pulls you farther from your *Warm Trait* and farther from God. When you are *Warm,* you can see the light.

The *Warm Trait* really requires no modification. It is not a karmic *Trait*. It is a relatively high vibrational state. It is the most connected trait to the spiritual world.

God would not modify *Warm* with *Air* because that soul would be so in their head that they would disconnect with the world, period. It is the connection with the world that provides us with our lessons and growth.

God would not modify *Warm* with *Fire* because *Warm* is already filled with passion.

God would not modify *Warm* with *Water* because God would not want the connection to the spiritual world muted.

And, God would not modify *Warm* with *Earth* because to be grounded in this case would pull you from the connection to God.

Once a soul reaches the *Trait* of **Warm** after many incarnations and is able to sustain that trait through not becoming conceited, jealous, selfish, or unforgiving, then God uses the two *Elemental* modifiers to help us on our archetypes or astrological signs. This is to aid us on our path. Once we have reached that level, God wants us to remain at that vibration, therefore providing us with the modifiers to help.

Because all lessons still need to be learned, an individual who is **Warm** can still experience an uncomfortable life. If it is necessary, God will modify the **Warm** *Trait* person with *Fire*. Because, in this case it is God's passion and compassion that is holding on to you.

**CRYSTAL – A person assigned the Crystal Trait has a karmic debt from a past life related to not trusting and not forgiving.** The **Crystal** has turned their back on someone in that past-life.

When you no longer trust someone, you can no longer see that person for who they really are. What is the correlation of the word **Crystal** and this tendency? Some cannot trust what they cannot see … it is not **Crystal** clear to them.

Unfortunately, with the **Crystal** *Trait*, there is a tendency to not trust the people in their life, not just the romantic relationships. The **Crystal** must learn to get past mistrusting people or else risk the chance of carrying the same karma to yet another reincarnation. If the **Crystal** person is able to overcome mistrust, they could return to their next life without this *Trait*.

The **Crystal** who is able to find another **Crystal** person, will find immediate trust. However, if that **Crystal** turns out to be untrustworthy and not who they were believed to be, the **Crystal** *Trait* will be lifted from the disappointed person and not follow them to another incarnation. There cannot be love where there is no trust. The **Crystal** is now self-aware.

Although the *Crystal Trait* is karmic, it is meant to be a gift from God to help draw two *Crystals* together to fix their karma in a trusting manner.

When you are *Crystal,* the light is refracted. Once you've overcome being *Crystal,* you can see the light.

Why would God choose to add the *Air Elemental* to the *Crystal Trait*? God would not. Because, mistrust begins within your head. This would further keep a soul in a mistrusting state.

Would God modify a *Crystal* with *Fire?* Yes, because if in this life two *Crystal* "Intendeds" are getting together, the additional passion created with the *Fire* will draw them closer together. And, God would know this before time.

Would God *Water*-down a *Crystal Trait?* Rarely, but yes. If a karmic debt with someone else in that life exists, that must be dealt with immediately, God could water down the *Crystal Trait* so the *Crystal* could still be with a non-*Crystal,* successfully. The mistrust is less, making it possible for a *Crystal* and non-*Crystal* to connect and address their past karma.

God would not choose to modify a *Crystal* with *Water,* if you will be in another life with your "Intended" because the connection must remain strong.

The *Earth* elemental would not be chosen by God for a *Crystal Trait* because being grounded in your mistrust of others would amplify the mistrust.

**RAINBOW – A rainbow has many colors as does the person given the Rainbow trait.** The colors of the *Rainbow Trait* person are their many colored Angels.

People assigned this *Trait* typically have nine different Angels surrounding them. Remember, this is a karmic debt *Trait*. Their Angels are to remind them of the debt they are working to overcome. This is a gift from God, meant to assist the *Rainbow* person.

Typically, each person is assigned two pink Angels to help overcome conceit, two green Angels in the attempt to conquer jealousy, two red Angels to remind them to forgive and two yellow Angels to help overcome selfishness. A ninth Angel is normally the Angel color of the *Trait* that is their biggest obstacle.

Why would God assign a **Rainbow** *Trait* to us? Usually, in another life a person was angry with God for whatever reason. But, like a loving parent, God would give us extra help in a new life to overcome any issues and hopefully find our way back home to God, permanently.

The pros of this *Trait* are that you are given lots of help! The cons could be if you do not get it right in this life, you may not be getting much help in the next life.

Consider this *Trait* a blessing even though it's karmic. God is giving this *Trait*, nine different opportunities for growth.

If you are **Rainbow,** and you realize you are seeing every spectrum of the refracted light, you also need to realize that all light comes from one source. The Source!

There is no reason to modify a **Rainbow** *Trait!* The **Rainbow** *Trait* has been given as much help as possible with all the Angels.

**ESOTERIC HIGHNESS – If God assigned this E.T. trait to a person, they turned their back on God, family, love and everything in a past life. Again, this is a karmic debt.**

God is saying to you with this *Trait*, "If you want to live without everyone and everything this time, you will live in your own head." Being assigned the *Esoteric Highness Trait*, they have difficulty thinking of anyone or anything other than themselves. They place themselves on the highest level of need and interest. That is the karma to overcome.

On a positive note, the *E.H. Trait* is very charming, friendly and nice. Therefore, people are drawn to them due to their welcoming nature and find them very engaging. Unfortunately, the **E.H.** person is always searching for someone to take care of them and their burdens. Jealousy and fits of rage are not uncommon to the person holding this **E.H.** *Trait.*

The **Esoteric Highness** person must learn to give of themselves rather than taking from others in order to overcome their karma. This is not a punishment but rather God making sure the person really learns to overcome and know the difference between giving and taking.

The person with **Esoteric Highness** has their head in the clouds. It is difficult to see the light through the clouds. If this person with **E.H.** can only see that life is not about them but about others, their head will no longer be in the clouds and they will see the light.

Although it may seem counterintuitive, God frequently modifies the **Esoteric Highness** *Trait* with *Air.* This is an attempt to raise them above the clouds in their head! It connects them to the vital force of *Air.* It connects them to life.

Never add *Fire* to **Esoteric Highness;** it passionately keeps them in their head!

Why would God modify the **Esoteric Highness** with *Water?* Well, God may modify this *Trait* with both *Water* and *Earth* together. *Water* in the clouds produces rain. And, rain falls toward the *Earth* nurturing the *Earth* and pulling the **Esoteric Highness** out of his head. The **Esoteric Highness** needs to be grounded and pulled out of their head.

**CAMEL'S HUMP – Just as the camel's back has high and low spots, so does this trait.** We previously talked about the Warm *Trait.* The **Camel's Hump** consists of the person's mood traveling back and forth from the Warm *Trait* to the Esoteric Highness.

God may have chosen the **Camel's Hump** for a person reincarnating because this provides a glimpse for that person about what being Warm feels like. They are normally too stubborn in their E.H., needing a constant reminder.

Interestingly, when the **Camel's Hump** is low and Warm, they are at their best, thinking of others and are the happiest. Unfortunately, they will not always admit it, but in this state, they do realize how much happier they are.

When on their high or in E.H. mode, it's all about their own needs and what makes them happy. While the Warm side is happy and content this E.H. state is discontent and agitated. The **Camel's Hump** is unaware they must harness their energy to stay in between or in the Warm state. Instead, many are depressed and have anxiety. Often, they feel the need to escape the reality of the E.H. state and medicate or self-indulge themselves as an excuse for their behavior.

Literally, in the **Camel's Hump,** God is trying to show you the light because you are too stubborn to see it yourself.

Using *Air* to modify the **Camel's Hump** would not be God's choice. It would push the **Camel's Hump** to the E.H. side and further into their head.

Does the **Camel's Hump** require the *Fire* modifier? Never. Adding *Fire* or passion to a vacillating *Trait*, would send them toward a volatile anxiety. God would never choose to do this. This *Trait* already has a karmic debt relating to volatility and God wants you to overcome this tendency or debt.

*Water?* Adding *Water* and *Earth* together to this *Trait* can lessen the E.H. because by grounding it does not allow them to stay in their head. Rain in the clouds brings them down and closer to the lower Warm **Camel's Hump.**

■   ■   ■

The first five *Traits* are directly related to finding and reaching for the light. Hopefully, you are able to recognize that the **Camel's Hump** is a transition from what is observable in nature as it references a camel and the search for the light. This difference is the separation between levels of energy from remaining in the lower aspect to evolving into the higher aspect of energy and, therefore, the light. These next *Traits* are descriptors based on what we see in nature to teach us lessons, helping us to grow and evolve.

**WILLOW – Why this trait, this time? The person given this trait by God turned away from their children, love or life in the past. Just like a willow tree swaying back and forth, needing to spread its branches and leaves constantly.** Karmically, in their past, they were escaping their responsibilities related to their actions.

A *Willow* must be nurtured because without it they do not learn responsibility as a nurturing parent would be. If they learn responsibility, they will overcome the karma of the *Willow*.

Being a *Willow* one feels the need to move, not stay put, go, run and not stick with anything. They also feel the need to move away, travel, change, change, change. They must overcome this behavior or receive a harder *Trait* in the next reincarnation. They must take responsibility around them in their current life. They must learn that the grass is not always greener elsewhere.

Thus, they will be drawn to those who nurture them. However, it is still their responsibility to learn from the nurturer. They will learn best from example. What they must remember to learn is that their needs are not the only needs of importance.

This *Trait*, the *Willow*, must learn to be selfless and responsible. That is the ultimate goal.

Does an *Air* modifier attach to the *Willow?* God would not choose to allow them to blow even farther off course.

Perhaps *Fire?* No!!! Because adding *Fire* to this tree (*Willow*) leaves nothing but ashes.

How about *Water?* *Water* can mute or slow down the desire of the **Willow** to run. And, the **Willow** does require some *Water* for growth.

And, does grounding the **Willow,** further its growth? Absolutely. The tree needs to stay put!

**ELEPHANT – The elephant is always plodding and making slow, thought-out, steady decisions.** *Elephants* by nature are smart, strong, slow but ever moving. They tend to their herd, being protective and responsible.

If you were assigned this *Trait*, in a former life you were squirrelly, making rash, fast decisions without considering the consequences. The **Elephants** tend to make good parents, teaching their children to think-out decisions and keep moving in the right direction.

The negative side to the **Elephant** *Trait* is that while responsibility doesn't bother them, they tend to take on too much responsibility making them exhausted at times and unavailable in relationships. Unfortunately, the **Elephant** also tends to be one-minded, stubborn and self-centered in relationships.

Consider this *Trait* to be a gift. You will naturally have the ability to take on responsibility unlike the Willow. However, there is a test related to this *Trait*. You are not the only person responsible in your arena of life. Your stubbornness and belief in only your way is conceited.

Should God add the *Air* modifier to an **Elephant?** They are already one-minded. They need to get out of their own thinking.

Adding *Fire* to this *Trait* can't make an **Elephant** move any faster. You can't light a *Fire* under the ass of the **Elephant!**

The **Elephant** does sometimes need to be muted with *Water.* It *Waters* down their stubborn tendencies.

Grounding an **Elephant** with *Earth,* because of a past karmic debt related to your children, gives you strong footing in overcoming your debt. Strong footing never hurts the *Elephant.* Without strong footing, an *Elephant* is even slower.

**SQUIRREL – The squirrel tends to make fast, rash decisions, not considering the consequences … often dead on the side of the road because they chose to make a run for it!**

This *Trait* is the opposite of the Elephant and most likely was assigned by God because in a past life you could have been an unsuccessful Elephant.

Although the *Squirrel* is a hard worker, they are too busy to think … always on to the next job. This debt or *Trait* causes one to be busy, busy, busy all the time. If not kept busy, the *Squirrel* will feel useless.

However, the *Squirrel* must make the time for their children and family. They could have parenting issues because of their need to be busy all the time. They may make the time to bake cookies or help their child build a Soap Box car, then, turn around and not take the time to attend the Soap Box Derby.

The *Squirrel* is a great worker and a multitasker, usually getting the job done. Sometimes they are off to the next job before the paint is actually dry!

The *Squirrel* must stop long enough to think about the consequences of their actions. Being busy all of the time can be a way to escape their own feelings and the responsibility of their feelings.

Those whose intentions that are almost always based on actions can be quite focused on the result. It's about what they can get. An example would be working for the outcome of material gain. The *Squirrel* wants material gain, yet doesn't take the time to think about the consequences of their actions later.

Sooner or later their environment will change to the point they will have to nest and hibernate giving them plenty of time to evaluate.

The *Squirrel* modifier of *Air* will always make them breathe, take a brake and contemplate.

Does the *Squirrel* really need more passion or *Fire* to keep busy? Heck no! Sometimes a *Squirrel* already creates enough heat in their whirlwind. If you add *Fire* to a *Squirrel,* you can make them too hot to handle.

Do *Squirrels* need *Water?* Sometimes, they require a bit of *Water.* But a *Squirrel* cannot swim as fast as they can run; so, the *Water* will slow the runner down!

Both *Water* and *Earth* can be attached to the *Squirrel Trait* creating a better parent.

Frequently, *Squirrels* need to be grounded with the *Earth* modifier; otherwise, they are flying *Squirrels.*

**LOON – The loon has a battle between nesting and taking flight.** Although the *Loon Trait* is attentive and takes part in the family, they are more likely to take flight if the life gets too difficult or something else interests them. And, usually, it will be with a wailing for themselves. Poor me.

One would be given a *Loon Trait* if in a previous life they turned their back on themselves. For instance, that person exhibited self-destructive behavior like alcoholism or committed suicide. They took flight from themselves. Coming back as a *Loon* makes one take a good look at "just how bad is it?" It is never so bad as to take your life which is selfish or abuse yourself with alcohol, drugs or food, just to cope. That is conceit to believe you need something besides yourself to help you get through it all.

If you have taken flight in your past lives, you will be tested again. Consider the gift. In the past, you may not have had a nest where you could remain. So, consider your nest before considering the flight. It's not all about you and you may be missing the support right in front of your eyes that, you seek.

*Loons* are very loyal to the home or nest. Their struggle is between being responsible to themselves and not wailing and complaining about how bad they have it.

*Loons* are territorial and do not mate for life. That's because they are still always willing to take flight if things become too difficult in the nest.

Adding *Air* to this *Trait* will send them off and flying!

Would *Fire* benefit the **Loon** as a modifier? In this case, *Fire* would add passion to the **Loon,** making it possible for them to mate for life.

Do birds require *Water?* Adding *Water* to this **Loon**ey bird gives them a peaceful swim, close to their nest. This allows them to watch over their nest without stretching their wings.

Is a **Loon** happy when they are grounded? They are, indeed, happy when grounded in their nest. Adding *Earth* as a modifier will satisfy the **Loon.**

## ANTEATER – An anteater goes along in their life, achieving only one task at a time, and in this case, it's eating ants.

Perhaps you were like Henry VIII in a past life. Perhaps you were larger than life and turned on everything and everyone. He was conceited, fought his wives, fought the church, fought about politics, always to get his own way. He went so far as to start his own church when he didn't get his way. He had his hands in everything around him and was busy, busy, busy, controlling everything and everyone. Perhaps in his next life, Henry VIII was made an anteater.

If you were assigned the **Anteater** *Trait* in another life you would be concentrating on only one task. You would be so busy paying attention to what you were doing that you wouldn't have time to control everything and everyone around you.

*Anteaters* are single-minded, therefore, completing each task before moving onto the next one. They are self-sufficient and not about attacking others in their path.

Unfortunately, an *Anteater* can become concerned with sustenance only … in the form of food and shelter or love and acceptance. Henry VIII indulged himself in everything even as a Crystal! Returning as an *Anteater* was a gift to help his indulgence.

The *Anteater* has a relatively tough outer shell and is not worried about outside threats. They live in an environment with plenty of ants for nourishment. Being an *Anteater* is a safe life filled with toil. So, maybe Henry VIII was cleaning commodes in his next life!

If someone was a bully in a past life like Henry VIII, making them an *Anteater* in another life wouldn't give them the ability to handle challenges while only being able to focus on the task at hand. Interestingly, Henry VIII was a Crystal as was Anne Boleyn. It should have worked. But he refused to trust.

Do you suppose God added *Air* to the *Anteater?* Yes. Adding *Air* to the *Anteater* can sometimes take them off the task at hand, considering others. Just maybe something else in life has importance.

*Anteaters* with *Fire?* There is no reason to make someone a passionate eater.

Can an *Anteater* drown? *Anteaters* are already docile animals … and ants cannot swim. The *Anteater* does not need to be muted or *Watered* down.

*Earth? Anteaters* do need to be grounded if they are parents. They must nourish more than just themselves.


**OWL – An owl is wise and smart. They can also be dangerous, skilled hunters killing for whatever they need.** An *Owl* can spin its head completely around, seeing and acknowledging everything around it, enabling it to be two-faced.

The person chosen to be an *Owl Trait* may be taking in a lot from everyone and everything but only choosing to see what they want to see.

They have stereo vision, meaning they focus only on what they see and not what is reality. Therefore, they don't appear to be near as dangerous as they are.

The *Owl Trait* person has the ability to see and understand in all directions, if they look and if they choose to. And, they must choose to see and understand it all, not just what they want to.

Remember, the *Owl* will kill and hunt for food and can turn away from you in an instant. However, the *Owl* is wise enough to know when he does it! The test or gift is that the *Owl* can choose not to turn away. Their struggle is to overcome their stereo vision. Using their wisdom so they can choose to admit that by their very nature, they are selfish.

An *Owl* is a bird who nests. Therefore, it possesses a sense of family. Choosing to nest with the family rather than constantly being on the hunt for adventure is the object.

Once the *Owl* realizes the purpose of the hunt, they also realize that the hunt's purpose is to feed their family.

Does an *Owl* require *Air?* An *Owl* who is never in their head will never learn their wisdom.

How does *Fire* or passion affect the *Owl* as a modifier? The *Fire* modifier should only be used on the *Owl* when the *Owl* is also modified with *Air.* The *Owl* who is not in touch with their own wisdom just becomes a passionate killer. An *Owl* in touch with his wisdom becomes a passionate provider.

This bird, the *Owl,* only requires *Water* to mute its two-sided nature. The example here is if an *Owl* was a Gemini. The Gemini, as we remember, has two sides to their personality. *Water* will mute their two-faced nature.

By their very nature, an *Owl* cannot be grounded because it would starve.

**MOTHER BULL – A mother bull can be protective, reliable, stable and capable of caring for its young no matter what.**

It's the dichotomy of the name really. The name is both feminine and masculine, hard and soft.

Perhaps in a previous life you turned away from your children. Being assigned the *Mother Bull Trait* will hopefully make you more attentive and protective of your children or family in another life. And, hopefully, one would become a strong and forgiving *Mother Bull.* They must overcome their tendency toward stubbornness. Obviously, you would have had a past life where you were not a good parent or protector.

A *Mother Bull* can also walk right over their young to get whatever they need and want, regardless of the cost. We've seen this in nature. It's apparent that the *Bull* characteristic means they believe they are the one in charge and ... to charge! There is a struggle within the *Mother Bull* to find balance between nurturing children and nagging everyone else.

The *Mother Bull* is not particularly delicate in a china shop, meaning they are not concerned with the wake they leave on their path. There is a struggle in their nature and their nurturing between allowing their children to think and demanding their children follow their thinking; stubbornly believing they are always correct.

Conceit is the test for the *Mother Bull.* They are great at mothering but never conceding to the failings of her/his nurturing.

Should *Air* be modified on a *Mother Bull?* NO. Sending the *Bull* into her head only reinforces their *Bull*ish nature.

Would *Fire* or passion benefit the *Mother Bull?* The *Mother Bull* is already passionate about her children. There's no need for modification.

Can *Water* mute the **Mother Bull?** Absolutely. Remember milk is 88 percent water. The **Mother Bull** requires it to retain her nurturing nature. This trait is always related to parenting karmic debt.

*Earth?* Although this is a nurturing *Trait*, in this case, the *Earth* just allows the **Mother Bull** to dig their hooves further into the ground.

■ ■ ■

After thoroughly reading through the twelve astrological signs and the twelve traits, one would expect to find recognizable attributes and characteristics with particular ones. We could turn a blind eye and pretend none of these describe us. But, what would we gain? How would we grow and evolve?

It would be more beneficial to self-evaluate and/or talk to our siblings or best friends and ask for assistance in finding our trait.

With each reincarnation both our astrological sign and our trait are chosen by God and our Spirit Guides to assist us on our path to gaining a higher vibration and getting back home.

Certainly, your personality has been self-determined over thousands of years. All of your previous choices and your reactions to them have been recorded in your soul. You bring this along with you to the next life along with your karma. Our choices on family mates, karmic mates, location and circumstance are very limited. We are given **either/or** choices or **yes/no** choices; again, related to how much we are willing to help others and overcome our karma all at once. It truly is a tough-love situation in order for us to learn and overcome. We may agree even though it is not our first choice ... because we understand that with the advice from our Counsel, God and Spirit Guides, we will overcome and assist others if making the correct choices to do so.

The specifics of our upcoming lives are not given in detail. We are given possible scenarios but really it is about whether our ego allows us to listen to the advice given. But, regardless, we are not given the opportunity to choose everything and anything as we please, regardless of what is written ... and we can never choose to avoid paying our karma. If we return with our ego intact, we must remember God modifies with the elementals at the very last, after we make our last and final choice.

God created us with yet another piece to our personality while on Earth. This part is ultimately decided upon by ourselves. However, we are advised by our Spirit Guides on the best choice. They hope we listen and take their advice. The third part of our makeup is called our *Archetype*. There are again twelve choices. This is the only definitive choice we make before we reincarnate.

## Chapter 11

# Archetypes ... Often, Written in the Ego

From the beginning of time, man/woman has tried to describe themselves. These patterns, much like the astrological signs, have been studied by religion, science and philosophy and these unique patterns are how men and women identify themselves. *Archetypes* are ego or self-identified roles. Just like in astrological signs and traits, what man/woman observe in themselves and others is usually what God purposefully created.

This allows man/woman a choice with each new life to identify themselves in a specific role. Again, this role is referred to as an *Archetype.*

There are twelve *Archetypes* to choose from when you reincarnate just like there are twelve traits and twelve astrological signs. These are all representative of the twelve faces of man or woman. In the case of choosing the *Archetype,* this time the man or woman chooses for themselves. As with all of our own choices, choices come with potential karma.

| ARCHETYPE | GOAL | FEAR | KARMA RELATED |
|-----------|------|------|---------------|
| Magician | Alter reality | Reality | Jealousy |
| Orphan | Belong | Exclusion | Jealousy |
| Creator | Create perfection | Imperfection | Jealousy |
| Innocent | Happiness | Punishment | Unforgiveness |
| Sage | Truth and Knowledge | Deceit and Lack of Knowledge | Unforgiveness |
| Lover | Connection | Isolation | Unforgiveness |
| Jester | Fun | Boredom | Selfishness |
| Rebel | Revolution | Powerlessness | Selfishness |
| Caregiver | To give | Be taken | Selfishness |
| Hero | Strength | Weakness | Conceit |
| Explorer | Freedom | Entrapment | Conceit |
| Ruler | Control | Loss of control | Conceit |

Above is a condensed chart listing all *Archetypes* in no particular order. They are divided into four groups of three which include their potential karmic debt if not overcome.

Goals are outlined as well as their fear, if the goal should not be obtained. Remember, fear is not possible with love. Therefore, if we live in love, fear will not exist. If we live in love then conceit, jealousy, selfishness and unforgiveness cannot exist and remember they are the roots of all fear and the roots of all karma.

Remember, at Atonement and before reincarnation, we discuss all choices with our Spirit Guide and God. This is the point when we decide upon our *Archetype.* We will be asked to consider all of our options, meaning *Archetypes.* We will be guided to make the choice which will bring us the most growth and evolution or serve others. But the choice is the only choice that is always ours alone.

**MAGICIAN – A magician creates an illusion.** The *Magician Archetype* would be suggested to a soul who is about to enter a life that is uncomfortable. For example, if a soul understands they could be born into abuse and would need tools to overcome the abuse and cope with the situation, and also, not have jealousy for those seeming to live a better experience, this would be the correct choice. Possibly, that soul was an abuser in a previous life, therefore karmic debt was created.

Another example of choosing the *Magician* as suggested by our guide would be if we were a victimizer in a past life. Possibly, we will be victimized in this upcoming incarnation. Choosing the *Magician* would cause us to face our reality if playing that *Archetype* to the ultimate level to overcome it. Or, we may choose to create a false reality. This would become our coping mechanism because to live in that true reality, we would be consumed with jealousy for those living a better existence. For some individuals, to be so poor and hungry could cause them to covet another's food and wealth. Much as the victim who chooses to feel sorry for themselves. But, choosing the *Magician* to avoid a challenge is choosing unwisely. We grow through adversity.

Sometimes the *Magician* chooses to manipulate the reality of their own and of others. For example, if we were with our "Intended" in a past life and it ended without love, we may choose the *Magician* in a next life, thinking we might manipulate the situation and win over our "Intended" according to our rules. After all, a *Magician* does not let the audience see what the reality is. They create a smokescreen to provide a new reality. The *Magician* can so alter their reality to the point of actually believing that altered reality.

The *Magician,* however, may be able to alter the reality of others to protect those others.

Having said that, creating a false reality can be a coping mechanism when it harms no one but helps the *Magician* to get through a difficult, abusive or victimizing situation.

Why would a soul choose the *Magician* if their Spirit Guide did not suggest it? Often, a poor choice is made in *Archetypes* when someone recalls their last life choice of *Archetype* that did not pan out. In this case, maybe that soul wants to continue to change and control their life and not be a victim or deal with the reality of it. Even awaiting another reincarnation, a soul has the tendency to create more karma for themselves when not taking the advice of their Spirit Guide. Their ego often believes it knows best. Remember, the Spirit Guide is here to help us but we ultimately make our own choices and karma. But, to choose the *Magician,* altering our reality and raising ourselves up at the expense of others, is still not the best choice; that indicates our jealousy of those we are competing with.

The *Magician* at its lower level creates a false reality for themselves, pretending to be someone more important and special than others. Operating at their higher level, the *Magician* faces their own reality and lives harmoniously within it.

Charles Manson was a *Magician.* He lured in members to his group with the false pretense of becoming a family. Then, he manipulated his family into his reality.

George Washington was the father of America and the first president. He was a *Magician,* and successful in creating a new world, and a new reality.

Would God modify a *Magician* with the *Air Elemental?* God would not! The *Magician* is already living in a reality of their own creation. It would not benefit the *Magician* to live more in their false sense of illusion.

Would *Fire* benefit the *Magician Archetype?* Applying *Fire* or passion to Charles Manson would have created a more passionate murderer. However, applying *Fire* to George Washington was the correct choice for God. He created a passion for inventing a new country.

God often applies *Water* to the **Magician,** muting the tendency to live a nonreality thus making the **Magician** live a more authentic existence. Again, using George Washington as an example, applying *Fire* and *Water* to his *Archetype* made George passionate in regard to change but not suicidal in war.

Is it necessary to ground a **Magician** with *Earth?* Sometimes, God uses the *Earth* modifier to keep the **Magician** grounded in reality. Grounding helps the **Magician** remember home and family. Otherwise, their false reality can take them far away from home and family.

**ORPHAN – An orphan has no biological connection.** Why would a soul choose to be an **Orphan** *Archetype?* There are two great reasons. The first would be for the connection to the family we are born into, which likely would be a short connection or life. This might be due to a karmic debt or for a lesson to one of those family members. Since the **Orphan**'s goal is to belong, the draw to that family is strong for that soul. Because it is not the purpose for the soul to fight the decision of an **Orphan** *Archetype*, knowing the life will be short. The goal here is more for the lesson to whomever than it is for the new **Orphan.**

Another case for choosing the **Orphan** *Archetype* would be for two persons to form a strong, family bond. In other words, a Spirit Guide would strongly suggest that a soul choose to be an **Orphan** so that they would bond with another already chosen **Orphan.** This could be due to a karmic debt or so that the two souls would form a wonderful relationship. Some *Archetypes* will bond instantly, where others may not. Imagine a scenario where one of the souls actually is an **Orphan** with no parents or family in that life. The other soul who has a family and parents would be very attracted to the **Orphan** and therefore the two become one and both have a family.

The Spirit Guides would suggest the **Orphan** for each of these particular souls because the two together would accomplish more than individually. And, if one or the other was meeting an early demise, the one left behind would not feel unaccomplished, knowing a truly loving relationship had come about. This would also speak to keeping their karma in cheque.

If two souls are uniquely drawn to each other as "Intendeds" the two together can endure hardships due to the strength of their relationship, easier than each could undertake alone.

The fear for the **Orphan** is exclusion and not belonging. This can result in karmic jealousy if they do not belong. Humans tend to covet what the others have and what they have not.

Why would a soul choose the **Orphan** if their Spirit Guide did not recommend it? For some, who have had an unhappy past life due to family abuse or violence from a group, they may assume they want no interaction and they'd be very comfortable being alone. That is never the case. A soul is not meant to be alone. It's all about the connections we make.

Choosing to be an **Orphan** *Archetype* against the advice of our Spirit Guide, based on our own ego is like asking for more karmic debt and to return yet again. We would've served no one's purpose including our own.

Remember, the reason for reincarnating is to rid ourselves of karma or to assist another with a lesson. Almost every *Archetype* is suggested for us for one of those two reasons. So, choosing an archetype for our own ego has no purpose and causes more karma.

Marilyn Monroe was an **Orphan** *Archetype* at her own request. That did not suit her ultimately, because the jealousy around her caused her own death. She wanted to belong yet always felt excluded, trying to climb the ladder to inclusion.

Joan of Arc was an **Orphan** *Archetype*. She had an extreme need to belong to her mission and the church. She gave her life rejecting church authority in favor of direct inspiration from God. She valued belonging to God more than belonging to the church.

*Air* modifying the **Orphan** could cause them to wallow in their "**orphan**-ness." *Fire,* however applied to the **Orphan,** can make them extremely passionate about belonging. Applying *Air* and *Fire* together, on the **Orphan**, fuels the *Fire*! It will almost ensure that the two "Intended-**Orphans**" will be drawn to each other.

There's never a good reason to modify the **Orphan** with *Water.* Why would God use *Water* to calm something that should happen passionately? Unless the soul went against their Spirit Guide's advice and chose the **Orphan** themselves. If a soul chose to be an **Orphan** *Archetype* and that placed them in an unhealthy family situation, God would not want the draw to stay in that family to be strong, should it be healthier or happier to be removed from that situation and family. Wanting or needing a family is never as necessary as being healthy, happy and loved.

Sometimes the *Earth Elemental* is used with **Orphans** because there is a need to be nurtured even if one doesn't find a place to belong; therefore, feeling grounded within themselves.

**CREATOR – One who creates by bringing something new or original into being.** The *Creator* brings about their own perfect vision of reality. They are quite artistically flared. Building and producing is keen to their happiness. However, the key to their happiness is perfection. And not seeing themselves as perfect but seeing others appearing to have reached perfection causes jealousy.

Why would a reincarnating soul choose the *Creator* as their *Archetype?* One reason to choose this type would be in opposition to the choice created for them in their past life. Literally, that soul would try to avoid the pitfalls of their last life by choosing to create this new one.

This is again an ego or self-driven thought. Often, the soul believes they deserve a better life next time and are envious of others who had. If the Spirit Guide feels this is the best choice, then ego isn't making the choice. Even though jealousy is the primary karmic issue with this *Archetype*, if we are ego-driven, we believe we can do better than the suggestions made by God, Spirit Guides and Counsel. The *Creator* in this case becomes conceited also.

The *Creator* who envisions in their mind the perfect life may have no tests or adversity to assist in growth. Then what is the point of this life, we ask?

Who is the perfect candidate-soul for the *Creator?* It's someone who in their past life tore down or ridiculed another. Why, you ask? Because, often the *Creator* has a vision and can pass their imaginative vision to that other person from that previous life, literally building them back up. This would help repair their karma together.

For example, a man we know from a previous life was a slave on the isle of Bermuda. He murdered and rabble-roused in retaliation causing more problems and hate for his people. In a life shortly after that one, he was a black man standing up and speaking out for his people. He was able during that life to spread his message in a positive way rather than by causing hate and death.

If using the *Creator Archetype* at the higher level, we can clear karma. Patience is a needed skill of the *Creator Archetype.* They must keep their eye on the vision and not focus on the imperfection that is still present. When focusing on the imperfection, they become jealous of the vision they have created.

Alexander the Great was a *Creator* and is best known for having conquered a vast empire that stretched from Macedonia to Egypt and from Greece to part of India. He was taken by all of the art painted of him and loved the flattery he received. He suffered from delusions of grandeur and had some belief that he was a deity. After his death, his empire crumbled. This is not the best example of a *Creator.*

Steve Jobs was also a **Creator** in this life. He worked tirelessly to coinvent Apple Computers. He worked endless hours to create his vision of how the public could be served through computers. He continued to be personally involved due to fear of his invention not being perfect. This is a great example of a successful **Creator** *Archetype*.

The *Air* modifier applied to the **Creator** causes self-evaluation which unfortunately leads them to more impatience; they wonder why they are not creating fast enough.

Does the **Creator** need *Fire* or passion? Yes, it facilitates change! If someone is meant to be a catalyst for change, adding the *Fire Elemental* will encourage their drive. However, applying *Fire* and *Air* to the **Creator** only encourages frustration.

Of course, applying *Water* to the **Creator** calms them if being the **Creator** was their choice and not the Spirit Guide's. Applying *Water* and *Air* to the **Creator** just causes a storm.

Applying the *Earth* modifier to the **Creator** reminds them of two things. First, that they must give attention to their family and second, that to create is not enough. The creation must still be nurtured. You can't make something new and just leave it to grow on its own. *Earth* will remind the **Creator** to remain strong and determined.

**INNOCENT – To be innocent, is when you are not responsible for or directly involved in an event yet suffering its consequences.**

Often when a soul returns as an **Innocent** *Archetype*, it is due to a previous situation that causes karma not completely of their doing. For instance, in our first book, we told the story of a young couple who were murdered by the Mob for trying to escape that life. In their next life, their Spirit Guides suggested they choose an **Innocent** *Archetype*.

Why? Because as an *Innocent,* a soul is often living a shortened life to serve others or comes as a miscarriage to another for a lesson. This is usually after that soul has forgiven the person in the past life who caused them suffering. They are aware that they are sacrificing themselves in the new life, to mitigate their karmic debt by serving others. They may also be advised to choose the *Innocent Archetype* as their lesson. In other words, possibly that soul had been unforgiving in a past life and a significant negative event is planned for their new life. They understand going into that new life, forgiving the event of suffering and returning to their goal of happiness, (their biggest goal) will erase their karma in that area. However, if they consider their negative event as some sort of punishment which is their greatest fear and are unforgiving, it will only add to their karma.

Example: You are living in a life where a close family member commits suicide or has a debilitating disease. You continue through life feeling sorry for yourself and do not evolve or grow but rather, spend your time reliving your perceived punishment. It has not been considered by you the possibility that the diseased-soul or suicide-soul could have eliminated or caused their own karma which really had nothing to do with you. Now, you have caused your own additional karma by pursuing unforgiveness.

Anne Frank was an *Innocent* and most known for her diary. She lost her life wanting only happiness and fearing punishment from the Germans. Unfortunately, Anne did choose this *Archetype* herself. Again, listening to our Spirit Guide is for a reason. They know best. She spawned unforgiveness against the Germans as a result of this life ... and more karma.

Does God suggest applying the *Air Elemental* to an *Innocent Archetype?* NO, NO, NO! This is so closely connected to karma that God would never suggest modifying it. There is plenty of existing karma already! Therefore, *Elementals*/modifiers would never be applied. God really is giving us chances to overcome.

SAGE – **A sage is someone who has attained wisdom.** The goal of the *Sage Archetype* is to attain truth and knowledge. On the flip side, their biggest fear is deceit or the lack of knowledge. In the case of the latter, a *Sage* would wallow in unforgiveness.

Why would a Spirit Guide suggest a *Sage* archetype to a returning soul? The *Sage* who seeks knowledge and shares it facilitates the growth of everyone.

Both Rumi the poet and Confucius the philosopher were *Sage Archetypes*. They successfully shared their knowledge and truth with the world. In fact, their published works are still shared with the world today. Of course, both Buddha and Jesus were also *Sage Archetypes*. Need we say more? Each of these *Sages* were forgiving people of their very own humanity.

Karl Marx is best known for writing *The Communist Manifesto*. Although he was also a *Sage Archetype*, he became obsessed with his own truth, blaming others for the faults of mankind. He believed that capitalism was a form of deceit, which was the opposite of the communist/socialist thoughts. His message to mankind was about conflict. He was extremely unforgiving of mankind.

Why would a Spirit Guide suggest to a soul not to choose the *Sage Archetype?* If someone had abused their role in a previous life as a manipulative ruler it would not be suggested to become a *Sage* where they would have knowledge to use to manipulate again.

When would God modify a *Sage* with *Air?* Only when the *Sage* had chosen this *Archetype* themselves, not listening to their Spirit Guide's advice. In this case, keeping them in their head lessens their effect on others. Becoming smart with knowledge and never using it with others is useless.

Does the *Sage* need *Fire* or passion as a modifier? Using Jesus as an example, remember that he was a *Sage Archetype* and went seeking knowledge throughout the world, sharing that knowledge with others. However, *Fire* was added to his *Archetype* not only to add passion to his seeking knowledge but also to add passion to his personal relationships.

Should *Water* modify the **Sage?** Sometimes it is necessary. *Water* can calm the already inflated ego. A **Sage** who believes their knowledge makes them somehow more special needs to be tranquilized with *Water.*

Nostradamus was a **Sage** of his choosing. He did not take the advice of his Spirit Guide, and as his ego was already inflated, God added the *Water* modifier to cool his jets! Without the *Water Elemental* attached to his **Sage** *Archetype*, he would have caused more karma for himself. We are not to predict the future or know our future. However, Nostradamus is best known for predicting the future. Because of his many predictions of disasters to come, Nostradamus had many more reincarnations to experience the disasters he so eagerly predicted.

Do we ground a **Sage** who is so eager to learn? Adding the *Earth Elemental* is unnecessary.

**LOVER – A lover is a person who has a strong enjoyment or liking for something.** In this case, the **Lover** *Archetype* craves an intimate connection with others. This does not mean necessarily as in a sexual partner or love affair. This is more correctly meant as a connection with people and the world. They crave a partner, family, friends and all types of close bonds.

The higher-level **Lover** connects and forgives. The lower-level **Lover** feels isolated and, therefore, has unforgiveness for those who have caused the isolation.

In what situation would a Spirit Guide advise a soul to choose the **Lover** *Archetype?* If a soul has been unforgiving in the past, it may be advised to choose this type and try again! Sometimes, a pair could be advised to choose the **Lover** *Archetype* because both will seek a strong connection, naturally.

And why would a Spirit Guide not suggest that a soul return to a life as a *Lover Archetype?* If a soul has negative karma with another and they are both reincarnating at the same time, however, they are not meant to end up together, making that soul a *Lover,* and the other soul a *Lover,* could interfere with the second soul's "Intended." The connection would be very strong but not meant to work out, making them both feel isolated and unforgiving.

Mark Antony and Cleopatra both chose against the advice of their Spirit Guides to be *Lovers.* They were not "Intendeds." It did not work out well, as Mark Antony first committed suicide thinking his lover was already dead and feared losing his power connection. Cleopatra was not dead, but later killed herself because she feared losing her connection to her throne and the people who adored her. These are not the best examples of *Lover Archetypes.*

Mumtaz Mahal was an empress of India and also a *Lover Archetype.* She died in childbirth with her fourteenth child. Her husband, Shahjahan, also a *Lover Archetype,* was so heartbroken that he was split from his love, he built one of the seven wonders of the world, the Taj Mahal, in her honor.

Does the *Lover* need *Air* to grow? Sometimes, the *Lover Archetype* needs a little *Air* to evaluate whether their love is being drawn to the wrong person. They apparently need time to think about their choice in lovers.

Is it ever suggested to add *Fire* to the *Lover?* Of course. *Fire* only creates much more passionate *Lovers.* And, of course, if they are "Intendeds" it's an added bonus. If both "Intendeds" have the *Fire Elemental,* one will need *Water,* so the passion will not burn them out.

Does a solitary *Lover* have the need for *Water?* Yes, to keep them from the negative choice in mates or family. *Water* calms the *Lover's* need for connection.

Is it possible to ground or make the *Lover Earth*bound? Since true love is never karmic, it is not necessary to ground the *Lover.* Having the need to belong to family or connect, would never be grounded or halted since that is the purpose for living. Connecting and loving is always the reason.

**JESTER – A jester was historically a medieval entertainer who relied on absurd humor.** The *Jester Archetype* can make fun of the world's hypocrisy. However, their main goal is to have fun. The main fear is boredom. It is easy to figure out that being selfish is most what the *Jester* needs to overcome and avoid.

Under what circumstances would a Spirit Guide suggest that a soul reincarnating choose this *Archetype?* In a past life, the soul was not serving anybody but themselves.

Bob Hope was advised to be a *Jester* and he listened to his Spirit Guide and agreed. He chose to make people laugh all over the world and included visiting soldiers during wartime without compensation. Thus, he overcame selfishness. This is a great example of fulfilling your choice!

Because many a truth is told in jest, sometimes the world needs to laugh at its own hypocrisy before it is even aware that it is hypocrisy. In this case, the *Jester* is serving the greater good. If you are instructed to choose the *Jester,* you are directly dealing with your past-life karma of being selfish. However, if you fail, you still have selfish karmic debt.

Robin Williams truly was a *Jester* in many ways, including as an *Archetype.* He actually chose this *Archetype* and made the world laugh. And, while doing it, frequently made the world think. Unfortunately, his struggle between having fun and boredom led him to the most selfish act of all.

Why would a Spirit Guide not advise a soul to choose not this *Archetype* of the *Jester?* By the very nature of the *Jester,* they seek attention by their antics, therefore, if they are choosing this

*Archetype* for fun, they are only serving themselves. Normally, with karma, one would choose an *Archetype* that serves others.

God never uses the *Air* modifier on the **Jester** because the **Jester** will just appear the buffoon. Unless the *Jester* has chosen this *Archetype* themselves. Then, God may choose to do so, leaving the buffoon with no one to entertain.

Does a **Jester** need more passion or *Fire?* Yes. Sometimes the world needs the **Jester** to make us laugh at the absurdity of this world and sometimes to even make us laugh at ourselves. Sometimes, laughter is the best medicine and a welcome distraction. Even God has a sense of humor.

Should God *Water* down the **Jester?** God frequently uses the *Water Elemental* and *Earth* to calm or ground the **Jester** *Archetype*. Because, life is never just about having fun. If someone chose this *Archetype* to just have fun, God would perhaps override it with a modifier.

The **Jester** may need to be reminded with an *Earth* modifier that it's not all about entertaining themselves.

**REBEL – A rebel rises in opposition against an established government or ruler.** The *Rebel* loves to cause upheaval or revolution. In fact, it's their goal. Because they fear powerlessness more than anything. The *Rebel* frequently acts against oppression and in that case it is selfless. However, should the *Rebel* choose to act out or revolt for their own purposes and gains, it then becomes selfish and their karma to repair.

Why would a Spirit Guide suggest the *Rebel* *Archetype?* Here's an example to describe those circumstances. Robert Gould Shaw was the colonel of the 54th Massachusetts Infantry, the first all-black regiment during the Civil War. He was advised by his Spirit Guide to choose this *Archetype*. He agreed. His parents being Abolitionists, he was familiar with acts against oppression. Although, in the beginning he was looking for glory, his purpose changed to his concern for the black soldiers having the same rights, value and pay as the white soldiers. And, as the movie showed, in the end, he stood by and for them to the death.

Why would this *Archetype* not be the best choice for a soul choosing to reincarnate? Perhaps a soul who had been in an oppressed group in a previous life would choose this with thoughts of uprising and retaliation.

One of the most successful **Rebel** *Archetypes* was Moses who was advised and chose to listen. He revolted against slavery of his people despite being raised by the Egyptian ruler who was enslaving his true people. He chose selflessness, knowing he would not find reward in going to the promised land. But he was successful regardless.

Do you suppose Moses had the *Air Elemental?* NO! It would have put him further into his head and, with that, ineffectiveness. If someone chose this *Archetype* and God believed it would be used incorrectly, then modifying the **Rebel** with *Air* would lessen their chance of being effective. During the Civil War, many of the southern leaders had chosen the **Rebel** *Archetype*. They were not necessarily fighting for their own rights but rather plain anti-establishment. They really just wanted their own way instead of wanting what was best for the greater good. God applied the *Air* modifier to many of these **Rebels,** knowing what their intentions would be.

*Fire* on a **Rebel?** Applying *Fire* on a suggested **Rebel** makes them more determined to accomplish their goals.

Applying *Water* to the **Rebel** *Archetype* may make them just go-with-the-flow. In this case, they may not fight for the change but they won't resist the change either.

If one chose to be a **Rebel,** does God ground them with *Earth?* No, because you would believe you are not grounded in your convictions. But, if God chose the **Rebel** for you, you may be grounded with *Earth* and, therefore, feel grounded in your convictions.

**CAREGIVER – A caregiver regularly looks after another.**
As a *Caregiver Archetype*, their need is to give to others but their fear is to be taken by others. That side of the *Caregiver* shows selfishness which is what they must be sure to avoid. The *Caregiver* must nurture as it is engrained in their nature.

Why should a soul choose the *Caregiver Archetype* when preparing to reincarnate? If that soul had been guilty of not being a nurturer in a past life, this is their chance to succeed in erasing that karma. In fact, they could be placed back into the exact or similar situation for a second try for improvement. Since this is totally karma related, do not assume it will be easy and simple this time around. You have past karma with someone, by your own hand, so expect to have a difficult situation to overcome. The other person may try to take from you, due to you taking and not giving in that previous life. Despite the major fear of being taken, this time around, the *Caregiver* must suck it up and be selfless.

If your Spirit Guide advises against you being a *Caregiver Archetype* it could be due to a previous life, when you enjoyed patting yourself on your own back. If your hope is as a *Caregiver* you will gain attention and look wonderful, your guide will most definitely not suggest it. This would be conceited and cause more karma.

Everyone knows the name Helen Keller and that she was blinded after Scarlet Fever but it's possible that the name Anne Sullivan does not ring a bell. Anne Sullivan was the woman behind the student. She taught Helen Keller to read braille, then to speak and actually helped Helen to write her own biography. She exceeded in *Caregiving* in the most selfless way.

During the COVID-19 crisis many nurses, physicians and other healthcare workers gave endless hours providing care to the affected patients. However, there were some who were actual *Caregiver Archetypes*, who decided to walk away from the job in fear of themselves being taken by the disease. Most of these healthcare workers went the extra mile while on the frontlines. Those who selfishly chose to walk away know who they are and must also realize their karma is waiting for them.

If the *Caregiver* is modified with *Elementals* whether you chose it or not, *Air, Water, Fire* and *Earth* make you better as that *Archetype*! So, maybe God will use them and maybe God won't! All of the *Elementals* add to the quality of the *Caregiver.*

**HERO – A hero is someone admired for courage, outstanding actions or distinguished qualities.** The *Hero,* above all else, needs to have strength and their greatest fear, of course, is weakness. How else could they be the *Hero?* If they are not strong enough to overcome, what is their purpose, they believe; without overcoming, they fear failure.

The *Hero Archetype* must feel he/she is overcoming an obstacle; an obstacle or a darkness, even if it is within themselves. Using their own personal strength is what is required to overcome whether for themselves or others. To believe they are only responsible for this action could lead to conceit. After all, we all have obstacles to overcome. Thinking you have some "superpower" and can somehow overcome better than another is when it becomes conceited.

Our Spirit Guide advises us to choose a *Hero Archetype.* Why? That could be the purpose possessing the drive to give of themselves and to others, possibly required from past karmic negativity. Perhaps in a past life we held another down. This could be our opportunity to reincarnate back with that same soul and this time be their *Hero.* Another reason one could choose a *Hero Archetype* would be due to blaming yourself during a past life. Example: Failure to a *Hero* is fear. If a soul failed in their own eyes, they may be advised to choose the *Hero.* This choice would hopefully aid in overcoming their fear of failure because to live in fear makes loving nearly impossible; that is, of yourself and others.

When should we not choose to be a *Hero Archetype?* First, if your Spirit Guide says not to it's for a good reason. For example, if you are choosing the *Hero Archetype* for admiration or reward, don't do it. That is conceit. Another example: A soul could be entering a life where someone else needs to be the *Hero* to fix their karma. Placing two *Heroes* together could set up an unhealthy competition ... both competing to be the *Hero,* leading them to conceit. This literally sets up one of the *Heroes* to lose. In any competition, when one person loses, they both lose. More negative karma is created at that point.

William Wallace, known as a Scottish Knight in the late 1200s, was one of the main leaders during the First War of Scottish Independence. He helped defeat an English army at the Battle of Stirling Bridge. (He was depicted in *Braveheart* by Mel Gibson). Wallace was a *Hero* archetype. He was advised to be a *Hero* and he accepted the advice. However, although he took on the cause and eventually was caught and disemboweled, he was the *Hero* for the people and not himself. This is a decent example of a *Hero,* but no one wins in war.

Not all *Heroes* are famous. We can be the *Hero* in our child's life. We can be the *Hero* in our families. Be there, work hard, be present for others and not only yourself.

A wonderful example of a modern-day *Hero* is Nelson Mandala. He gave his life to the cause. He spent years in jail to support his people. He was asked by his Spirit Guide to be a *Hero* and he selflessly agreed. He was not a proponent of war just a change in the darkness of the society he lived in.

If *Air* is applied to the *Hero Archetype* when choosing it themselves, their fear of failure is amplified. Almost always this leads to their actual failure. If they cannot overcome their fear of failure, they will create for themselves ... more karma.

Does a *Hero* need more passion or *Fire?* If you have chosen to be a *Hero,* not listening to your Spirit Guide's advice, you may be modified with *Fire*. But it will come as no surprise if you burn out. However, if you were advised to choose **Hero** as your *Archetype*, modifying with *Fire* will certainly make you a success!

If you choose to be a **Hero** against all advice, you may be modified with *Water*, twice. In this case, you will be swimming upstream and may even drown.

If the **Hero** is a recommended choice and you will be facing significant opposition, God may modify you with *Earth* to provide you with strong footing.

**EXPLORER – The explorer archetype is independent and adventurous on a quest to discover.** The quest to discover can be a spiritual quest. It doesn't have to be to discover the world and new things.

The need to explore and the desire to not be entrapped can make the *Explorer Archetype* restless. Being restless is conceit. This means you want to meet your desires instead of meeting the wants of others in your life.

When would a Spirit Guide advise you to choose the *Explorer Archetype?* Two **Explorers** can do well together. They can support each other's need for adventure. If that were the case, neither would feel entrapped by the intensions of the other. Their quest may lead them to a new sense of purpose, even at the hand of adversity. Of course, this is probably working toward ridding oneself of karma.

For example, Rear Admiral Richard Evelyn Byrd Jr. was advised to choose the *Explorer Archetype* when reincarnating. He took the advice of his guide. He became the first American naval officer and explorer to reach the North Pole and South Pole by air. He also trained Charles A. Lindbergh (famous for flying nonstop from New York to Paris) in navigation and in the use of specially extended runways for landings and takeoffs. Admiral Byrd is a wonderful example of an *Explorer Archetype*. He used his discoveries to advance navigation and the science of survival in extreme temperatures in flight and on the ground.

The *Explorer Archetype* could become obsessed in their quest of discovery which lends itself to conceit. Literally, it would be an attempt to have a pat on the back for their bravery. They could also become conceited enough to believe they could take on any challenge.

What would deter a Spirit Guide from advising one to choose the *Explorer Archetype?* If the person reincarnating already has tendencies toward noncommitment. If a person already had karma from a previous life where they did not commit fully to a relationship or circumstance for whatever the reason and exhibited conceited tendencies, this would be more than sufficient reason to not choose the *Explorer.*

If a soul needs to learn how to become a team player or part of a group such as the service, being an *Explorer* isn't the correct choice. *Explorers* love to take off on their own adventures and spend time alone. If someone is dependent on an *Explorer Archetype*, more than likely they will be disappointed.

An *Explorer* may also lead a group into danger not considering the outcome for the group but rather fulfilling their own quest. Jim Jones, leader of the Peoples Temple, coerced his followers to Jonestown, Guyana, convincing them that "revolutionary suicide" was the way to go by drinking Kool-Aid mixed with cyanide. So fearful of entrapment, Jones himself committed suicide by a gunshot to the head.

Adding the *Air Elemental* to the *Explorer Archetype* only increases their daring nature. Their only fear is confinement or control. Because, when the *Explorer* looks out into the *Air*, they can see no walls. The last thing that the *Explorer* wants to do is hold their breath; holding their breath makes them feel confined to their body. They have the need to keep moving on. God may add *Air* to the **Explorer** that chooses this trait. They may take unwarranted risks if not controlled by their choices and actions.

Is it practical then to add more passion or *Fire* to the **Explorer?** If the **Explorer** had been recommended by a Spirit Guide then *Fire* will add passion to their adventurous nature. For example, if climbing Mount Everest was a goal, the **Explorer** would be ever so more determined to reach the top of the mountain. However, *Fire* used on someone who chose this *Archetype* themselves may make them more passionate about their chance to fail. It may paralyze them into taking no action. God would have been applying passion to the fear in that case.

Think about the daredevil who believes they can attempt anything and achieve! God could be saying to that **Explorer:** "If you choose to jump out of a plane without a parachute, don't be surprised to hit the ground and splat!" Remember, the *Archetype* we choose should be under the advice of our Spirit Guide.

The **Explorer** *Archetype* whose future will include the probability of *Water*, in exploring the oceans, for example, requires the *Water* for the comfort, because an **Explorer** that views the world from under the *Water* sees walls surrounding everywhere. The feeling of walls around the *water* is limiting because the **Explorer** feels no *Air*. Rarely, except for karmic situations, will God modify the **Explorer** with two *Waters*. The feeling of control from the *Water* will drown the **Explorer**.

Many people have fear of drowning, coming from past-life issues and many souls that have felt controlled choose the **Explorer** *Archetype* even if it is not recommended. They are attempting to run away from the control instead of facing it. By adding two *Waters* to the soul in this situation, God is saying, "Do not be conceited, for fear is conceit. If you do not face your fear, you will drown. If you go for it, I will help you. You cannot run or hide from your karma."

Would God choose to modify an *Explorer* with *Earth?* If the *Archetype* was chosen under the recommendation from a Spirit Guide, God may modify this *Archetype* with *Earth* to keep them closer to home and family; especially if the family has karma with you, you with them, or you still need to be reminded of your responsibilities. In this case, God is giving you a little extra help, making your need to wander feel a bit more grounded.

**RULER – A ruler archetype has dominion or control over others.** Some may take this role as responsibility or a mission to take care of others. However, some may take this role because they believe they know best. There's where the conceit karma kicks in.

What the *Ruler* wants more than anything else is control and their greatest fear is loss of control. At times, a Spirit Guide will suggest that a soul waiting to reincarnate becomes a *Ruler* because that person needs to learn control of self. Here's an example: A soul has karmic debt related to self-injury by drug addiction in a past life. They had loss of self-control in that life. Choosing to be a *Ruler* in the upcoming incarnation can heal that karma if able to learn to control themselves. Escaping into drug addiction, or alcohol or any addictive behavior is normally because their conceit has allowed them to believe they need not feel any pain or disappointment. They literally feel entitled to relief.

Another time a Spirit Guide might advise this *Archetype* is if the individual is committed to improving the welfare of those he controls or guides even to the point of self-sacrifice. Both Gandhi and Thich Nhat Hahn, both *Ruler Archetypes*, became *Rulers* to serve others. These are beautiful examples of this choice. There was no conceit related to the service they gave.

When would a Spirit Guide definitely not suggest the *Ruler Archetype?* A person who has abused power in a past life could have the tendency to continue on if becoming a *Ruler Archetype* in their next life. Like in the case of Nero, the last ruler (Roman Emperor) of the Julio-Claudian dynasty is best known for abusing his power as one of the worst emperors ever and burning Christians alive, causing the greatest fire in Rome and devaluing Roman currency. He killed his own mother and many family members and as a final act, asked for someone to kill him, finding no volunteers as he was the last of his dynasty. He then attempted to force his secretary to kill him to avoid an unpleasant death later. He eventually took his own life. His Spirit Guide had advised him not to choose a *Ruler Archetype.* He previously had karmic debt related to power and control. His choice was in error yet again creating much more negative karma.

The *Air* modifier may be a good choice for the **Ruler** *Archetype* if the **Ruler** in the past had a tendency for making rash decisions. This would tend to make them have thoughts "in their head" before making decisions. Adding two *Air* modifiers to the **Ruler** who makes this decision without the advice of the Spirit Guide will keep them so in the head, they will make no decisions at all. They can control no one and not even their own thoughts. Choosing the **Ruler** *Archetype* based on your own ego, God may make all of your decisions and choices ineffective. Thus, you cannot correct or overcome your karma. You'll probably be creating more karma on top of what you already carry to that life.

*FIRE* with a *RULER?* It seems like a bad choice, however ... both Gandhi and Thich Nhat Hahn were modified with *Fire* creating incredible passion to help others. God would never modify the **Ruler** who chose this *Archetype* against the advice of their Spirit Guide with *Fire* unless God wanted to ensure an uprising against the **Ruler.** The people would rebel against the tyrant-**Ruler.** If you were a tyrant-**Ruler** in a past life and you chose without consideration again to be the **Ruler,** God must ensure that you will fail at being a tyrant and that the oppressed in the past have a chance to overcome their karma. Example:

Nero, a **Ruler** with a *Fire* modifier, became so passionate about control that he literally burned part of his own kingdom, destroying what he chose to control, as mentioned a few paragraphs ago. Nero displayed ineffective leadership through his control, injured thousands and reincarnated with even greater karma. He reincarnated to Persia in AD 200, living on the edge of the Lut Desert as a servant boy. Literally the hottest place on Earth. That's a bit of tongue-and-cheek karma. Nero burned people to death in one life and ended up returning to a life where he burned from the sun and heat in daily living! His sole job was to fan his owner. During the hottest point of every day, his owner would tell him: "It's too hot for you to fan." Nero, then renamed Kaleb, lived his karma but learned a valuable lesson from his owner which was compassion.

■　■　■

If you examine the *Archetypes*, in almost every case there is a test related to choice.

Before each and every life, God gives us freedom; freedom to choose part of our path. In each case there is an option to choose love and forgiveness over conceit, selfishness and jealousy.

Will we choose to serve ourselves or choose to serve others? Did we learn anything from Atonement where we were shown all of our past lives and our shortcomings? Did we listen to the advice of our Spirit Guides or remain fixated on our own agenda?

Now that we have discussed our astrological signs, our traits and our *Archetypes*, we should discuss how these are chosen once again.

God, the great architect, has a plan. This plan includes which of the souls we will reincarnate with, be it family mates or karmic mates. This also includes when, where and who we will be born to. We do not make that decision. Again, God chooses our astrological sign and our trait. Our *Archetype* is the only choice that is ours to make. However, that choice should be in accordance with the advice given by our Spirit Guide.

We do not have infinite choices despite what some schools of thought have suggested. But we may have received alternate choices from God, Counsel and Spirit Guides related to our reincarnation.

For example, we are preparing to return with our soul group or family mates. We may have more than one karmic issue to be dealt with. Our choice to deal with one karmic issue over another may affect the new life we are given. Let's say we only want to deal with the karma created with our former husband. However, it is suggested that we also bring in a former family mate with whom we also have karmic debt. Our advice from God, Counsel and our Spirit Guide could be that we include that other person in this life; killing two birds with one stone. Consider, when life sometimes seems to be one lesson after another, it is because we went along with this choice and agreed to it. We have options but we do not make all the decisions.

It is possible that you can or cannot deal with two karmic debts in one life. God may not think you can handle it or it is possible that your karmic mate is not ready or within the cycle of your reincarnation.

Let's explain this further. We may have significant karma with our father from a past life. But we died young. Our father in that life may be eighty-five-years old on the day we were reborn with another incarnation. He dies at ninety years old. Would it even have been possible for you to correct karma with a man of that age? It wouldn't be fair, and as a five-year-old, not possible. That ninety-year-old must go through *Atonement* or a *past-life review* which could be instantaneous or in your perspective, it could be one hundred years. That father must also choose again, with the assistance of his Spirit Guide, the karma he has created, which needs to be repaired.

Both souls must be in cycle and available to each other for karma to work. That is why when exploring our past lives we do not always find the same family mates available. And, that is also why when we pass over not all of our family mates are present to greet us.

Back to the dodecahedron and our Pods. Visualize a three-dimensional flattened sphere, related to the fourth dimension which is time, according to Einstein. Time is based on the observer. And this description is based on the observer that is in the earthly plane. Time has no meaning in the spiritual world. Consider the center of the flattened, spherical grid or dodecahedron. This center is the tunnel experienced by NDEs (near death experiences) and through meditation and in past-life regression memories. We all return to the spiritual world through this metaphorical tunnel. It is the same metaphorical and actual tunnel we use through reincarnation or new birth. Return to your visualization of the dodecahedron or grid. Now visualize all points of the grid turning, involuting and rotating within itself, all occurring around the tunnel.

Those family mates or karmic mates that are not in Atonement reach the tunnel at the same time. Thus allowing them to return or reincarnate at approximately the same time. Those in Atonement miss this cycle. The cycling is consistently varying. That's why time between lives seems to vary. This is why as you do past-life reviews you may find someone in your lives twenty times or six times. Yet, without a doubt, you understand they are family mates or karmic mates.

■    ■    ■

## Chapter 12

# Lessons ...
# Written in History

Napoleon Bonaparte was born under the *Sign* of **Leo** on August 15, 1769. He was best known as a French military leader/emperor who conquered a great deal of Europe during the nineteenth century. He was said to be a shrewd and ambitious military strategist, skilled in waging war successfully against many European nations in order to expand his empire. It is estimated that two million civilians were killed during his marches.

Being prejudiced against everyone who was not French, he reinstituted slavery during his reign, using much of the conquered land's people. He literally believed them not to be as valuable as his French people.

Earlier in the nineteenth century, the French colonies of Saint-Domingue and Guadeloupe were having large slave rebellions. Napoleon was in charge of stopping the rebellion, which he did, brutally. It is written that he ordered his troops to concoct an extremely poisonous gas from nearby volcanic burnt sulfur, using the holds of ships as gassing chambers.

History records his death as due to stomach cancer while in exile from his country. The island of exile happened to be located off the coast of Africa.

Although Napoleon was first married to Josephine, he was known to have multiple mistresses. He divorced her to marry another woman.

His *Trait* was the **Squirrel,** so he would have concern for all the things around him rather than being just single-minded. He had the need to be busy and keep moving. He chose the **Explorer** as his *Archetype* against the wishes of his Spirit Guide. He was advised to be a **Hero,** choosing to be strong or weak. Being an **Explorer** would keep him moving and away from his responsibilities. His concern was the need for adventure instead of his family and responsibilities.

In a previous life, Oajdi (Napoleon Bonaparte) had been an **Anteater** *Trait*, single-minded and only concerned with his own nutrition … feeding his own soul, that is. It would not have been abnormal in that life to eat first and feed his wife and children second. He was extremely jealous in this life. Therefore, as Napoleon, he was given a green Angel from Raphael's legion to help with jealousy. And, is it any wonder that Napoleon died not having the ability to have food in his stomach, as Oajdi had eaten it all?

Oajdi thought he had failed in this life, during his life review, specifically failing his children. So, therefore, in the life as Napoleon, it was suggested that he choose to be a **Hero,** hoping he would have the strength to choose to give of himself to his children and wife. Instead, he chose to be an **Explorer** avoiding his personal responsibilities once again. Oajdi had sold his own African people into slavery in this life. The first person he sold in that life was a man who showed interest in Oajdi's wife. The jealousy was rampant.

Oajdi had been a large, overweight tribal leader, whose tribe rebelled. His last memory before he died was being told to run as fast as he possibly could. As he waddled away, he was pummeled with spears from his entire tribe for what he had done to their people. The spear that pierced his heart and took his life was thrown by his wife in that life and she was also his wife in the next, Josephine.

God modified the **Squirrel** *Trait* as Napoleon with the **Earth** *Elemental*, hoping to keep him grounded and closer to his family. It was unsuccessful. By him choosing the **Explorer** *Archetype*, the need to busy himself was amplified.

After our life review, while God, our Spirit Guides and Counsel are planning our next reincarnation, we are not aware of the choices made of our **Astrological** *Sign* and our *Trait*. Knowing we are returning for either karmic reasons or to help another, we should understand that the choice of our *Archetype* can affect us in a dramatic way. Taking the advice of our Spirit Guides is suggested for a reason. They know best.

God modified Napoleon's **Leo** *Sign* with the **Earth** *Elemental* again, to ground him and keep him with his responsibilities. It did not work. Remember, sometimes when you believe you are the king, someone has to kick a little dirt (**Earth**) in your face.

Consider that Oajdi was a selfish and jealous man who was not good to his wife, children or tribes people and, therefore, was placed back with that same wife in his life as Napoleon, given an Angel to help with his jealousy, given modifications to ground him to his responsibilities, chosen to be a **Leo** whose tendencies can be as great leaders, placed in control of an army, advised to be a **Hero** to his family and French people, yet abused the power once again.

In his next life, as a **Cancer** *Sign*, although this sign is family oriented, they fight the tendency to be conceited. Oajdi and Napoleon both displayed great conceitedness. God then returned him as a **Cancer** under the *Sign* of conceit with the conceit Angel from the legion of Chamuel to help him.

Juan, his new name in that next life, was from Spain. Of course, Napoleon had invaded Spain and had to learn a lesson in Spain in yet another life, as Juan.

Juan returned in this life as a **Loon** *Trait*. Remember, the **Loon** is a nester with their family. **Cancers** are also family minded. God gave Juan more help again in this life. But he still had karma in Spain to overcome.

Juan lived during the time of the dictator Franco. This is a time of oppression for the Spanish. Remember, Napoleon and Oajdi enslaved people. It is karmic for Juan to live what he caused others to live.

In this life, Juan toiled endlessly without reward. He was told to choose **Caregiver** as his *Archetype*. He listened to the advice of his Spirit Guide this time. His **Loon** *Trait* was modified with the **Earth** *Elemental* again. He learned in this life to feed his children before he fed himself.

Juan's daughter in this life in Spain was also his daughter as Oajdi in Africa.

Unfortunately, Juan could not completely overcome his conceit. He believed he deserved better in life than what he had. He led violent riots against the dictator Franco. Standing up to oppression is admirable, however, the nature of the violent rioting caused suffering and death to many. He soon died at the hands of the oppressors, leaving his children and his wife to fend for themselves. His fight was for himself rather than his family and country. It is no surprise that Juan is now living again. He has been reincarnated as a **Libra** *Sign* presently. And, hopefully, as a **Libra,** he is weighing his choices better this time along with his Angel of jealousy, Raphael.

■　　■　　■

Cleopatra VII was the last active ruler of the Ptolemaic Kingdom of Egypt. She was born in 69 BC under the *Sign* of **Libra.** She had been declared a joint ruler of Egypt by her father, along with her brother, Ptolemy. **Libras** notoriously crave equality and are notoriously jealous.

She was advised to choose the *Archetype* of **Sage;** however, she chose **Ruler,** again, the carry-over from her last choice.

Her political position and that of her son Caesarion (with Caesar), was much more important to her than love.

Her spoken language was Greek, which was the language of the educated people of the time. Her position gave her the right to enslave and control. Yet, Cleopatra was not from Egypt. She was born in Macedonian, Greece. She was a descendant of Alexander the Great, who had conquered Syria and Egypt.

Her strength was not in her beauty, in fact, but rather her intellect. She first married her own brother Ptolemy XIII to retain power. He attempted to take her control, because Cleopatra attempted to control the throne completely. She regained control by joining with Julius Caesar. Once Caesar defeated her brother in battle, he drowned him in the Nile.

She then married her younger brother Ptolemy XIV again to have complete power. She arranged the murder of this brother again and the execution of her sister. Both siblings were in line for the throne and Cleopatra wished for her son Caesarion, to corule beside her.

Her relationship with Mark Antony actually occurred during her relationship with Caesar. She needed his power to help protect her control while Caesar was elsewhere. She gave birth to three children with Antony.

Caesar made it known that Cleopatra was his mistress which inflamed all of Rome never acknowledging their son, however. She actually stayed in Rome in lavish quarters, paid for by Rome. She then returned to Egypt and married Mark Antony. The scandal raged in Rome. Octavian, Mark Antony's Roman rival, called Cleopatra a scheming seductress and Mark Antony a traitor to Rome.

Cleopatra used sex as power to control the men who could help her maintain her position. Although she did not think herself particularly attractive, she knew control could come in the form of seduction. In fact, she actually withheld sex to get exactly what she wanted. Once she got what she set out for, killing was not out of the question. Cleopatra actually wore a hair comb with snake venom in one of the tines. She would stab the comb into her intended victim, if necessary. During sex, Cleopatra always wore her comb in case the end desire was to murder. She had a deep-seated fear of men, therefore, wearing her comb she always had protection against men. Cleopatra believed the men around her wanted her power or her body, never respecting her mind. Her jealousy was toward anyone with power or better looks. She enjoyed having flamboyant entrances dressed in her most luxurious attire or jewels.

Cleopatra's *Trait* was that of the **Camel's Hump.** Apparently, in her previous life, she had the **Warm** *Trait*. Which meant she was connected to God, could talk to God, when open to listening. However, she was changed to the **Camel's Hump** in her next life as Cleopatra. If you recall, the **Camel's Hump** is between being **Warm** and **Esoteric Highness.** Being **Esoteric Highness** means who are stuck in your own head and struggle to think of anything other than yourself.

The life before Cleopatra, Roxana had been married to Alexander the Great against her will after he conquered her lands. Remember, Cleopatra was Greek and took control of another land, Egypt. In a previous life, her lands had been conquered, thus Cleopatra conquered land not of her own.

Roxana had been born under the *Sign* of **Capricorn.** After the death of her husband, Alexander, Roxana killed off both of his first and third wives. She had a son with Alexander and wanted no competition from his other wives. Unfortunately, Roxana and her son were murdered by a competitor later on. **Capricorns** have tendencies toward unforgiveness and are concerned with their money and control.

We first see that Roxana carried many soul traits along with her to the life as Cleopatra. Being returned as Cleopatra under the *Sign* of **Libra** was to remind her to weigh her choices of right and wrong. And, being returned as the **Camel's Hump** *Trait* was to place her a bit more in her head to think. God also modified her *Trait* with the **Air** *Elemental* so she would evaluate her actions. God additionally modified Cleopatra's **Ruler** *Archetype* with the *Elemental* of **Water** in an attempt to calm her fear of loss of control.

Roxana was an incredible beauty! Cleopatra was not; karma … and God expected Cleopatra to not use her body for power but rather her mind.

Roxana chose the **Ruler** *Archetype* but had been advised by her Spirit Guides to choose **Caregiver** to care for her son and her people, who had been conquered by her husband. However, she chose **Ruler,** deciding to take care of herself and her son (power). The modifiers that God gave her had no effect, unfortunately.

Roxana had been controlled. Cleopatra's goal was not to be controlled. Therein lies her karma. However, Cleopatra was not meant to be control----ling! Her own ego negated the opportunity to overcome Roxana's karma. Roxana's people had been conquered, however, Cleopatra learned nothing from that experience and continued to conquer others.

The next life for Roxana/Cleopatra was in Mandarin, China, as Min. It was around AD 240. Min was the daughter of the last Han Dynasty Empress's illegitimate son. She had no power during this lifetime. Her father had wasted all of the material wealth bestowed on him from his mother. Min had not used her power in her two past lives in a beneficial manner.

Min, as an adult, owned only two sets of clothing.

She was born under the *Sign* of **Aries,** placing her right back in her head … to think! However, God modified it with the **Earth**

*Elemental* to ground her. She adapted but remained jealous of her father her entire life due to his squandering of their wealth. She chose the *Archetype* of **Magician,** although her Spirit Guides had advised the choice of **Sage.** Again, using knowledge to further herself, rather than being consumed with money and power was the object. She, of course, wanted to **Magically** create her own reality. God modified her again with the **Camel's Hump** *Trait* with **Fire.** The hope was to ignite her **Warm** side once again, as in her life as Roxana. When you add **Fire** to a **Warm** *Trait*, it's to ignite their passion. Because, in her past two lives, she had no interest in passion but rather power.

Who we are … seems to follow us. God is trying to give us help; however, we don't always listen.

■  ■  ■

Anne Boleyn is best known as the mistress of King Henry VIII of England while he was married to Catherine of Aragon, the Queen. The king was having an affair with Anne's older sister Mary at the same time. Catherine's ability to not provide the king with a male heir caused him to seek out another woman to bear his son and heir.

Henry was denied a divorce from the Catholic church which began the English Reformation and, in other words, the start of the protestant Church of England. He eventually received an annulment from the church he created and married Anne Boleyn.

Anne was born in July of 1501 under the *Sign* of **Cancer. Cancers** possess tendencies toward moodiness and despondency, and in Anne's case it was due to her inability to produce a male heir. She did, however, give birth to his daughter, the first Queen Elizabeth. Anne was extremely jealous of her "lady in waiting," Jane Seymour who wore a picture of Henry around her neck. Henry VIII was also a **Cancer** *Sign* which should have drawn the two even closer.

Anne was given the *Trait* of **Crystal,** as Henry was also a **Crystal** *Trait.* Let's recap what the **Crystal** *Trait* means. That *Trait* is given to those souls who, in a past life, mistrusted a mate. Anne and Henry had been in a life, previous to this one, because … they were indeed "Intendeds" or meant by God to meet. Additionally, Anne and Henry were advised to choose **Lover** as their *Archetype* which would have pulled them even closer to one another. However, Henry chose **Ruler** and Anne chose **Lover.** God modified both of them with **Fire** and **Water** on their **Crystal** *Trait.* This should have ignited their passion, which it did, and the **Water** was to cool their tempers and so not to burn each other out which it did not!

Because Anne did not produce a male heir for Henry, he began to search for reasons to rid himself of yet another wife. Only three years after their marriage, he set out on a campaign to prove Anne to be unfaithful, incestuous and a conspirator. This time, Henry VIII had his wife beheaded so that he could marry his third wife, Jane Seymour.

It should be noted that the swordsman responsible for the beheading of Anne was of French descent. In their previous life, Anne and Henry had been French themselves.

The swordsman, in their previous life, had had an affair with Anne. This swordsman had been in many previous lives with Henry and Anne and in each case, was responsible for having affairs with either Henry or Anne which led to the ultimate demise of Henry and Anne's relationship each time.

In the life before Anne Boleyn, she was again named Anne. She was not royalty, however. She had been married to a French soldier named Pierce (aka Henry VIII). He was part of a French and Spanish envoy during an attempt to unite their countries. It had been an ill-conceived coalition. As an Englishmen, Henry VIII despite his marriage to the Spanish Catherine of Aragon, was also part of an ill-conceived coalition with the Spanish against the French.

During Pierce's absence, his wife, Anne, encountered another French soldier which ultimately lead to an affair of the heart and bed. Henri (French for Henry), her new love, was spurned on Pierce's return. Interestingly, he beheaded her in his next life.

Anne had been born under the *Sign* of **Capricorn. Capricorns** tend to believe they are correct in all matters, believe they are the most proficient at their occupations … which in this case was a cook for King Charles VIII where she had met Henri, and **Capricorns** always long for a relationship with security. During the time of Pierce's absence, Henri was a higher-ranking soldier. However, when Pierce returned, he was rewarded with a commendation for his service, making him higher rank than Henri. Anne ran back to Pierce to enjoy the benefits of his promotion. She was already with Henri's child and Pierce knew it was impossible to be his. It was, indeed, a son but not Pierce's son.

Anne's son grew and as a near adult, Pierce trained him as a soldier for the French army. Pierce "accidentally" killed Anne and Henri's son during training. This explains why Henry VIII could not seem to bear a son that lived. As Pierce, he would not accept a son and, therefore, in his next life as Henry VIII, he could not conceive a son that lived. Interestingly, Pierce killed the sixteen-year-old boy as a soldier, and his son with Jane Seymour, as Henry VIII, lived only until the age of sixteen.

During this life, Anne's *Trait* was a **Mother Bull,** who is typically more interested in having the child for means than making the child for pleasure. Anne had been given a red Angel in this life under **Capricorn** for unforgiveness, however, she never did forgive Pierce for the death of her son. Her *Archetype* was **Caregiver** which had been advised by her Spirit Guide. This brought her even closer to her son/responsibility.

Usually, a shared responsibility between two people, like a son, would bring them closer together; however, Pierce chose **Explorer** *Archetype* over the recommended **Caregiver.** Of course, he did not step up to care for a child but rather kept moving. Pierce was also born under the Sign of **Capricorn,** which should have again brought the two closer. He was also given the red Angel of forgiveness to help them forgive one another to no avail. Both Pierce and Anne had entered this life also, as the **Crystal** *Trait.* Neither learned to trust each other in this life or the one following as Henry VIII and Anne. God had modified Pierce and Anne with the **Earth** *Elemental* on their *Archetypes* and **Fire** to both **Crystals** to ignite the passion. As you can now see, God will give as much help as possible but choice and free will ultimately cause the result.

Following their life as Henry VIII and Anne Boleyn, the two were reincarnated together yet again. You see, God does not give up on us. He gives us chance after chance to learn and grow.

Their next life, Anne was Henry's daughter. Because God hoped that the love they would feel together as father and daughter would not be related to emotional passion but rather a family bond. However, they were still born under the *Trait* of **Crystal,** hoping to form a trusting bond together. Realizing that at this time in England, the taxation from The Church of England (that Henry VIII created) was oppressive. This removed the opportunity for this father and daughter to have financial abundance. Henry had unknowingly created this for his next life.

Priscilla and Johnathon were the daughter and father of a normal peasant family. Priscilla married a man named Henry, who also happened to be a **Crystal** *Trait.* Henry worked as a blacksmith and was quite adept with tools and creating weapons, like swords (a big ha, ha).

Interestingly enough, Johnathon had given his daughter's hand in marriage to the same man who had used a sword on her head in their previous life. Priscilla never had a brother and Johnathon never had a son in this life. However, he did have a grandson, who was the reincarnation of Henri's and Anne's son in their life together in France. This was just God's gentle reminder. In other words, Priscilla once again gave birth with Henry (Henri) to the same son. In this life, Johnathon's (Henry VIII's) blood did run through his veins.

The relationship between Johnathon and Priscilla was that of closeness. They had trust and respect for one another as father and daughter. Once Priscilla's husband Henry moved the family to the New World of America, the relationship waned as Johnathon stayed in England.

Priscilla sent but one letter to her father for the duration of his life.

Priscilla was born under the *Sign* of **Cancer** in this life, of course, making family an important tendency. Her *Archetype* and that of her husband were both the **Explorer.** Both having this *Archetype*, that had been advised by their Spirit Guides, almost assured that Johnathon would feel the loss of his daughter and grandson as they traveled to the New World. It also gave Priscilla and Henry a common goal which bound them together.

God had modified Priscilla with the *Elemental* of **Earth** on her **Cancer** as did Henry on his **Pisces,** as did their son on his *Archetype* of **Explorer** as well. This brought their family together. Priscilla and Henry were also modified with **Fire** on their **Crystal** to ignite their trust.

Johnathon's wife, Priscilla's mother, had died very young in that life. Oddly, she was the only wife he had. His previous life as Henry VIII had brought him many wives.

Johnathon was buried with the one and only letter from Priscilla. He considered it his prized possession.

Johnathon's sister, who cared for him until the end of his days, was none other than the reincarnation of Jane Seymour. The woman that Henry VIII professed to love more than any of his wives, was now in a position to care for him only as a brother. Jane Seymour saw Henry VIII as her savior and financial goal in life. And, in this life, Johnathon was a burden for the rest of Jane's life.

Ludwig van Beethoven was born in December of 1770 under the *Sign* of **Sagittarius. Sagittarians** are inclined to become intellectuals or pseudo-intellectuals, finding enjoyment in the sound of their own voice. He is best known for his musical composition. He is considered to be one of the greatest musical geniuses of all time. He came from a family of German musicians.

He composed over the last ten years of his life, without the ability to hear. He became a social recluse due to his lack of hearing in public. Although, **Sagittarians** can become a bit reclusive under any circumstances. Wanting an audience is essential to them, to share their intellect.

There is a great tendency toward jealousy which makes it difficult if their partner is also an intellect. It is not odd then that Beethoven never married. He could not tolerate a greater intellect than his own.

Although a great composer, he lacked the gift of becoming a great student. Beethoven was also partially dyslexic which added to his concern but actually added to the unconventionality of his music. He imagined his music when others as well as himself could not hear it. His *Archetype*, which was advised by his Spirit Guide, was a **Magician.** He **magically** created his own reality, even though he could not hear it. Apparently, Beethoven had been given the **Willow** *Trait*. This provided him the tendency to need nurturing. His father was relatively abusive verbally and an alcoholic which did not nurture his *Trait*. The **Willow** has a knack for turning away from either their responsibilities and/or their wife and children. So, apparently, Beethoven displayed this behavior in a past life and, therefore, felt it in his life as Beethoven.

Hoping to gain acceptance from his father, Beethoven pushed his genius with his music and his father, in turn, pushed his son to be a musical genius. Unfortunately, Beethoven's father pushed him to perform at a very early age of about six years old. His musical talent was not completely developed at that young age and, consequently, his gift was not acknowledged by the public at that time. Therefore, his father pushed much harder for his son to become the best.

Around the age of twenty-seven, Ludwig contracted typhus which is related to bacteria from fleas and rats living in your area. If not diagnosed and treated promptly, it causes long-term hearing loss in a percentage of persons. Ludwig lost his hearing. His mother had died when he was just seventeen years old of consumption (tuberculosis). He was forced to receive a court order at the age of eighteen for his father to continue to support him. After the death of his mother, his father would only support his music. He paid to send him away to learn with other great musicians such as Mozart and Haydn. Typhus was in an epidemic state at that time.

God had modified Ludwig's **Magician** *Archetype* with **Fire** and his **Sagittarius** with **Fire.** Igniting passion in his *Archetype* helped him become a more prolific creator of music and adding **Fire** to his *Sign* of **Sagittarius** actually made Ludwig more independent which he needed without nurturing from his father. Being the **Willow** *Trait* was karmic for him from his past life where he refused to be nurturing in his responsibilities.

Although Beethoven was not religious despite being raised Roman Catholic, he did not attend religious services but made several well-documented references to his faith in his music. His string quartet numbers revealed the evolution of his music and as a man.

Ludwig van Beethoven in his previous life had been a Muslim man named Ahlmed. Per their tradition, when his brother died who was his father in Beethoven's life, he accepted his brother's family into his home. However, he treated them as less important than his own; literally feeding his own family and himself before feeding his brother's family. Is it any wonder that as Beethoven his father was not willing to support him? Although he lived two opposing religious sides, he did not partake seriously in either.

When Ahlmed's wife told him that his brother's wife and children were starving, Ahlmed chose to *not listen.* He struck his wife. It is no wonder then, that in his next life as Beethoven, he lived an abused life with loss of his hearing. Ahlmed continued to degrade his wife for bringing to his attention the needs of his brother's family. This type of behavior was not spoken aloud. Therefore, when Ahlmed went to prayer services, the other men would not speak to him.

As Ahlmed, he was meticulous and always well groomed. However, because of lack of nurturing as Beethoven, he bathed infrequently and was nearly always unkempt. This karma is directly related to Beethoven contracting typhus. Ahlmed had been born under the *Sign* of **Libra** and when his wife reported to authorities that her husband had struck her, he was very concerned how it would look to others. **Libras** are notoriously concerned with how they look and how things appear. The unkempt appearance of Beethoven only added to the reasons he never had a wife. His arrogance regarding his gift in music also made him appear unattractive in his boastfulness. Additionally, Beethoven's karma, created in his life as Ahlmed, led to him not having a wife or family.

Ahlmed had been assigned the *Trait* of **Squirrel,** to work and provide for his and his brother's family. That was a gift from God. His **Squirrel** had been modified with **Earth** to ground him to his responsibilities; more help from God.

Beethoven had been a **Willow,** rooted in the ground. Had he been nurtured he could have been a good family man. God additionally modified Ahlmed's **Lover** *Archetype* with the *Elemental* of **Fire** as he did for Ahlmed's wife, Miriam, to draw them together. Ahlmed and Miriam had previous life-karma together and were in this life to overcome that karma together. Because of the violence that Ahlmed had shown toward Miriam, he was drawn into his next life as Beethoven with his mother who had been Miriam who died when he was young. This left him to be abused at the hand of his father.

Under the *Sign* of **Sagittarius,** Beethoven was provided an Angel to help overcome his unforgiveness. He was to forgive himself as Ahlmed in his previous life and his father in his life as Beethoven. He was also to forgive his wife as Ahlmed, for reporting him, who was now his mother as Beethoven. Unfortunately, Beethoven harbored anger toward his mother for dying young and not protecting him. Losing a mother young makes a man awkward toward women as an adult which ensured that Beethoven would remain unmarried and alone.

The life after Beethoven, Joe was born under the *Sign* of **Taurus.** God modified his **Taurus** with the *Elemental* of **Water** to calm his tendency toward anger. His given name was Undah. Joe was an African slave born in The United States at the time of The Civil War. He had been born this time to two very loving parents. His older sister when he was Joe, was his mother as Beethoven. He was again given the opportunity to heal the karma between them. His sister was extremely nurturing as a **Piscean – Caregiver.** She was his chief **caregiver** while his parents worked the fields. Joe would ask his sister Bessie (given name Bowah) to sing to him daily to which she complied. Joe complimented her as she sang.

This soul had been dark-skinned, then white-skinned and now dark-skinned again as Joe. We live all sides to learn.

His *Trait* was that of the **Loon,** modified by **Earth.** The **Loon** stays close to the nest and **Earth** grounds him additionally to his responsibilities. The test for the **Loon** is always whether they will decide to take flight if responsibilities become too tough. Joe chose his own *Archetype* on the advice of his Spirit Guide. It was the **Hero. A Hero** can choose to be weak or strong. In his situation as a slave, it would have been strong to stay and weak to leave.

The Civil War was coming to an end. Joe's sister's husband was killed. Joe was expected to assume the responsibilities for his sister and children. Remember, as Ahlmed, he begrudgingly helped his brother's family.

As a **Taurus,** Joe stubbornly decided he would not fail. He cleared a small area of trees and built a cabin barely large enough to accommodate his family and his sister's family. He share-cropped cotton with many other former slaves. He planted and raised his own garden. He worked a side job with another white farmer when it was time to butcher the farmer's meat. His payment was in meat only to feed his and his sister's family. Joe traded his vegetables for chickens. He trapped rabbits and squirrel when he could not provide meat. His hard-working nature did make Joe a **Hero** to his family.

Song had always been important to Joe. When his sister Bessie died, he taught Bessie's children the same songs their mother had taught him as a child. It wasn't until he was much older that Joe understood the meaning of his people's spiritual hymns his sister had taught him. Joe continued to sing on perfect pitch until the day he died.

Joe also forgave his sister for dying young. He sat on her death bed and thanked her for everything she had done for him. Joe had learned a lesson in love, but certainly, it was not a love for all. Because Joe never quite forgave the white slave-masters who had beaten him and taken and killed his sister's husband. He did funnel his anger in a positive way into his work. His conceit as a **Taurus** despite having an Angel to assist him, allowed his unforgiveness to continue and to remain prejudiced toward his oppressors. On his own death bed, he judged himself more worthy of a place in Heaven than his previous white slave-owners.

■ ■ ■

It could appear that the *Signs* and *Traits* chosen for us and *Archetypes* we choose do not reflect our best qualities or abilities. It could seem critical or a very harsh manner to place us in these different types of *Signs* and *Traits*. However, they are chosen to ensure we actually face and learn our lessons. Or, if we do not overcome our karma and learn our lessons, we will be reincarnated once again under new *Signs*, *Traits* and *Archetypes* to try and overcome again. It is not, however, for us to judge. Judgement is God's alone.

Not only must we face our karma, but also we are assisted in realizing and overcoming our karma. God still tries to help us by giving us modifiers, Angels, Spirit Guides and advice on *Archetypes*.

*Signs*, *Traits* and *Archetypes* affect approximately 30 to 40 percent of the outcome of our lives. Environment affects about 10 to 20 percent. Free will is responsible for the rest of the percentage in the outcome of our lives.

God gives us help and tests. We are placed into the environment where we will grow and evolve. However, our choices while incarnated have the majority of the effect on our karma.

### Elizabeth, Isabella and Mother speak ...

Love flourished as Katrina and Giovanni gave birth to six children. Many grandchildren came from their six children. After the story of the teacup when Gabriella was four, Giovanni carved a twelve-inch-high, wooden stool. The back of the stool was fashioned with a handle which was two feet from the ground. Katrina used the handle to support her weight in rising from the stool. The stool was created so that Katrina could spend time close to the floor with her children and then grandchildren. Katrina's mother, Ms. Orsini, embroidered the cushion that covered the seat.

**Love, Elizabeth.**

■   ■   ■

One of Giovanni's favorite memories was the Christmas he gave Katrina the little stool. He watched as she laughed and played with the children on their level, not hers. Her playful nature became evident in every aspect of their lives. Gio would even catch her singing when she was by herself with no one to hear. She continued to sing and as the grandchildren arrived, she taught each of them to sing, all seeming to possess the gift of voice. The grandchildren grew and it became more difficult for Katrina to rise up from her low, wooden stool, regardless of the handle. The stool was then relegated to the corner of the living room. Every time Giovanni glimpsed at the stool in the corner, he became flooded with beautiful memories.

*Love, Isabella.*

■   ■   ■

Daily, Katrina would gather a basket and her crutch to make her way to the market square. She would shop for their fruits and vegetables for that day, sometimes meeting her mother at Horatio's fruit-and-vegetable stand. Horatio noticed that both women were struggling to carry home their baskets of goods. That particular day, Horatio thought to himself … or at least he thought it was his own thinking, one woman is struggling because of her age and one is struggling because of her infirmity. He thought, "I will call on Giovanni and express my concerns." So, the next day, he visited Giovanni and explained his observations. Giovanni was aware Katrina did not want her disease to define her. The next day, Giovanni walked home from the apothecary at noon and accompanied Katrina to the market, carrying home the filled basket. That day, he smiled one more time at the little stool in the corner, as he carried it back to the apothecary. He carefully removed the embroidered cushion and placed it as a seat cushion on the rocking chair he had made for his mother-in-law, Ms. Orsini. He placed the rocking chair in the place that formerly had been reserved for the little wooden stool. The following day, Giovanni hired the driver of a red-and-gold carriage pulled by two white stallions to escort Ms. Orsini and her belongings back to their home where she would live out the remainder of her days with their family. Upon sunset that evening, Giovanni carried Katrina to the carriage, and as they rode, it reminded them of their first official alone date, and as they held one another's hands as on the first date, they remembered the love they had shared and the plans they made so many years before.

*Love, Isabella.*

■　■　■

Just a few years later, Giovanni noticed his wife struggling to walk up the hill with her crutch. He mentioned this to his mother-in-law. He said that soon Katrina would be unable to make the trip to the market. Ms. Orsini worked her way over to sit in the rocking chair. She said, "I have felt quite at home here. You have provided a wonderful home for myself and my daughter. I'll not be needing this rocking chair much longer. She pulled out a gold piece and told Giovanni, "I believe if you take this and the rocking chair, you should be able to purchase an appropriate wheelchair for Katrina." Ms. Orsini then handed her son-in-law the embroidered cushion. This cushion has carried both of us and should continue to carry Katrina. Giovanni purchased a wheelchair and placed the embroidered cushion on Katrina's seat; from Mother to daughter and daughter to mother, then mother to daughter ... in love.

*Love, Mother.*

■　■　■

Each day just before noon, Giovanni announced, "Katrina, your carriage awaits." He then pushed his wife down the hill to the fruit-and-vegetable market in her wheelchair. And, each day Katrina would stand up with her crutch to pick out the fruit and vegetables. On all of those days, Giovanni would take Katrina's hand to escort her back into the wheelchair so she would never fall again. And, on every one of those days, Katrina would say, "I find as much joy holding your hand in this carriage as I did on our first date." Giovanni then pushed her back up the hill to home. This continued until their last carriage ride.

*Love, Isabella.*

## Chapter 13
# Atonement ...
# Written in Our Karma

What happens when the incarnation is finished in our present life? Immediately, the soul disassociates with the body. A guide will assist us with our metaphorical journey. This will occur in a way that comforts us. For some, the transition is more difficult. Changing our perspective from the physical to the spiritual can be confusing. All make this transformation. Our guides form a personal visualization that eases this transformation. In all cases, we will travel through time, space and eternity and we will reach the light.

This is not a trap ... this is a welcomed relief for everyone.

No soul is lost to wander confused or disoriented. Our guide is present at every step of the transformation. God leaves no one behind.

The visualization that eases our transformation may include holding the hand of a loved one, one last dance, the song of an angel, a comforting memory, a favorite experience. It may be the chance to feel the fall of one last apple tree, if you were George Washington.

Why are some transitions difficult? Because, sometimes it feels that the opportunity to complete the lesson has ended too abruptly. The soul already recognizes that it did not complete every lesson that was assigned.

Sometimes the soul clings to its own ego. What if I am not accepted? Because I have not reached my potential. But that never happens. We are greeted by our family mates, with open arms. And in the open arms of our family, we again feel the warmth and love of God.

After transition, the soul is aware that it is close to home. We then find ourselves surrounded by twelve loving souls. They are called our Counsel. We are guided step by step through a past-life review that is filled with compassion and love from Counsel. Every lesson is taught; even those lessons that were incomplete. We will feel the compassion for every karmic debt that we created with others. Then, we will reconcile each and every intention of every action with God.

Then, a new cycle will begin. A plan or plans will be placed in front of us. These include our birth, family, tests and karmic challenges. There will be obstacles to overcome and assistance in overcoming them. The assistance comes from family mates, Spirit Guides, Angels, our astrological sign, our trait, our elementals and possibly our choice of archetype. The obstacles are karmic mates, our astrological sign, our trait, our elementals and possibly our choice of archetype.

After Atonement, we return to our Pod to contemplate our life review that we created with our karmic choices in our past life or lives.

Although our Pod is comfortable, still within the presence of God, we are aware that the distance from God will become greater once we reincarnate again. We are also aware that the veil separating us from the communication with God is the same veil that protects us from the sense of loss of God.

We then feel the energy moving in and upon itself. We are suddenly limited by our physical reality. There is flow and once again, we are gasping for breath. We have life, limits, potential and possibilities.

## Life Review or Lives between Lives ...

### Dave

I have been fortunate enough to have experienced time in Atonement during this lifetime where I examined my past lives and what I needed to work on in my next life.

I stood metaphorically in front of a group of teachers or Counsel as they called themselves. The members of Counsel all had previous lives but had finished their paths and no longer needed to reincarnate. I had first gone to a "holding place" while waiting to face Counsel. We now know that this is known as the second plane and Counsel and Atonement are on the third plane. We will explain all of the seven planes shortly.

There was love emanating throughout the room. I first felt confused because I experienced great light coming from them (especially their eyes). And, when I say experienced, I don't want it to sound like I really saw something, it was as if I just knew and felt what was happening.

Then, it was like I was watching a movie of my past lives. I was shown errors in judgement and poor choices I had made. I had hurt or injured others, either mentally or physically. I felt the other person's discomfort or pain. And, then I felt disappointment in myself.

As I stood there in the room before Counsel on the third plane, I felt great light and love and did not wish to leave. Yet, the light grew farther away and all I wanted to do was return to the

Godly light. Counsel talked to me about my choices and made me aware that I had to wait until the time was right for me to return to Earth and my next life.

I then felt that I transitioned. I was in a familiar place. It also existed back on the second plane. I felt warm and safe. Light shone and reflected in all directions around me. The lights were colorful and emanating in every direction. As the light reflected off of the edges of the twelve-sided dodecahedron and each of the five edges, it resembled crystals. When I say light, I mean that I was feeling the light.

I was connected to all others who had to wait also within our Pods. We had no wants or needs. We could watch or feel what was occurring on Earth. I tried to reach out to those I knew on Earth because I was still tied to that Earthly world. Every once in a while I thought someone heard me. So, I spoke even louder. Yet, I got no response.

I sat and thought about how I had to do more before I could feel that beautiful loving light from God. I was suddenly warm and floating. I was safe but wanted life. I felt the flow of water and blood around me. I breathed my first breath; it was cold and I cried. At that moment, all I could feel was that I wanted. I was back on the first plane of Earth.

I have also experienced that moment after death, several times. The hand of a young, dark-skinned little girl took my hand and pulled me up through light, time, space and eternity. I knew that hand for that little girl had died in my arms twenty-seven hundred years before, during my sixteen reincarnation. Since that time, she has been at my death, holding me until I began to again recognize those with me on the other side. I was dazed, and no one could hear me for I could not speak. I had no physical body. Yet, those around me were trying to comfort me. And, at each time, then again, I was before Counsel.

I've been shown portions of my father's Atonements or rec-
onciliations with God on different occasions. His life review was
also like my experience at that time with Counsel and Atonement.
There was an Earth plane, where we all lived. Then, we transitioned to the second place to wait for Atonement. Then, there was
Atonement, the third plane. The Atonement plane had greater
energy and more of God's love. Then, we went to a lower energy
plane and we waited in our Pod, our home, with reflecting light
all around, twelve sides; Reflecting the light from God but farther
than we had been from God during Atonement. We sat there
wanting to be so much closer to that light.

One night, after again watching a past-life Atonement of my
father's, I watched my father's final Atonement after which he rose
to an even higher plane. He ascended to what we call "Over the
Horizon" which is the place we go when our lives are finished and
never have to reincarnate again. This is the fifth plane.

The fourth plane is the place souls remain to either perform
a job for God such as gatekeeper, animal caretaker or past-life
guides (not to be confused with Spirit Guides) and Spirit Guides,
I have learned. And, yes, this is the plane that all of our past-life
animals reside. They do not reincarnate because they have no
karma. Animals obviously have consciousness, however, because
they have no karma, they have no soul. The soul is the depository
for our karma, only. Indeed, animals go over the rainbow bridge,
to their special homes on Plane 4. Animals are pure love, living
on instinct.

My father later visited me and with his metaphorical arm
around me told me that we all want to go, Over the Horizon, on
Plane 5.

During the experience of my life review, I was given thousands
of choices though I seemed to be guided to only one choice. In
each of my last three lives I chose the Archetype ... Innocent,

and died as a child once, then twice died as miscarriages. These were meant to be a lesson for others of forgiveness. My only real choice was to choose the Archetype. Isabella, my Spirit Guide, sat with me and guided me on my final choice. I could choose any Archetype I wanted, however, if I wanted to serve God, I was to choose the Archetype of Innocent, she said. Just as Isabella has done in all forty-two of my lives, she has attempted to guide me in my choices as all Spirit Guides do.

### Katrina and Giovanni's Life Review at Atonement; Their Counsel speaks ...

At her last breath, Katrina felt Giovanni's hand. It was still strong as she had always remembered it. Her mind was whirling. She felt a small hand grasp hers. She thought, "Gabriella," then, remembered Gabriella was full grown. She looked down to see a small, dark-skinned hand holding hers. She realized she was no longer standing on her withered leg.

Suddenly, lights flew by. She was in a red carriage with gold trim, pulled by two white-winged stallions. She thought the hair on her arms must be standing erect and felt as if her skin was literally electric. Katrina tried to speak but could hear no words. It was as if there were stars and crystalline light just out of her reach. She felt her mother call her name. Then, she felt immense energy and knew the *energy* was calling her name. However, she did not recognize the name. She thought, "I am Katrina" but the *energy* was calling her Ariela. Every time the *energy* called her name, she again felt electrical as if she was connected to that *energy*. Her vibration was rising to meet that *energy*. The *energy* calling her name was bathed in a royal-purple color, she felt. She tried to reach for the color yet could not move.

The purple Angel cradled her. And, she felt peace. Beyond this, it appeared as if a crystalline mountain range formed the horizon. Beyond that were thousands of points of light. Those points of light, shown in all directions, except one singular point of *light* that shined directly at her. That *light* lifted her. It was for a brief moment she thought the *light* was stronger than her Giovanni yet the love was familiar. The love grew stronger and at that second, her vibration raised once again. She recognized the *light* and the *light* was filled with love. The *light* spoke even though there were no words, "My child, Ariela." At that moment, she recognized the *light* was God. Three days had now passed.

She found herself in a metaphorical hall. Twelve wise beings of light were present. She caught a glimpse of her very first life as Ariela. She was proud of her beautiful garden. And, then she was shown and asked a question. "Why were you too proud to show your leg, as Katrina? Aren't both of those signs of conceit; boasting over your garden and being too proud to show your leg? There is a difference in humbly being pleased and being proud," she heard. "You made someone feel their garden was less than yours thus they felt inadequate and in this life as Katrina, you overcame feelings of inadequacy because of your leg. Be careful with every decision. Karma is present." Other lives flashed before her and more lessons followed. At times, she asked herself, "Why would I have made such a decision?" Each time, the answer was conceit, jealousy, selfishness or unforgiveness.

She viewed her last life as Sussan; she saw herself poison a man and then experienced the wails of mourning it caused an entire country. She heard, "The man you poisoned had no chance to learn or correct his poor choices. You were jealous of what you lacked or no longer had because of that man." A calm, authoritative voice spoke, "Justification is mine. I will not condemn the victim of an atrocity who was a child and had no choice. She showed love and compassion to a broken man and their children. Jealousy must still be overcome but there is no karma accumulated in this death."

Katrina had been born at God's decision as a **Libra** with jealous tendencies. However, God gave her the green Angel of

Jealousy, which was Raphael to help her overcome. But she was advised by her Spirit Guide and Counsel to choose the *Archetype* of the **Orphan.** Because the **Orphan**'s goal is to belong which would mean the need to belong would outweigh any conceit she would have had due to the position of her family in that life. Yet, she would need to feel what it was like to not have a father, because the man she had poisoned was, indeed, someone's father.

Therefore, in her life as Katrina, she had no father yet she had a mother who taught her etiquette and what was proper. She was then placed in a position to meet a young man who challenged her in a respectful, proper manner. If she could overcome the conceit of her family position and the jealousy of her **Libra** *Sign* that young man, born an **Aquarian,** which made him strong enough to challenge her, born under the *Archetype* of **Caregiver,** could actually have nurtured her.

As Sussan, she had been controlled. However, societal expectations were upon Katrina to marry and be taken care of which could have been misconstrued as being owned once again. Although Katrina attempted to have her disease not define her, it did without any control by her. Consider that there is selfishness in allowing someone to care for you. But that was not the case for Katrina, either by society or by her malformation. God believed the need for Katrina to not be jealous was more important than being under someone's care. She took her independence where she could, despite her disability and societal expectations.

If we examine many of her past lives, she and most women were *always* owned throughout history and in the case of most men, due to the time in history, most of those men were owners.

It may seem a fine line but there is a difference between being expected to be a good mother and wife and choosing to be a good mother and wife.

Katrina was assigned in her next life to be born under the *Sign* of **Aquarian** as Sarah. Additionally, she was advised to choose the

**Lover** *Archetype* and so she did. She returned to Plane 2 and to her Pod where she would ponder her past life and lessons, awaiting her new birth.

■  ■  ■

A few years later, Giovanni went to bed one night. He laid his hand like he did every night, where Katrina once laid. He said, "Good night Katrina," and imagined her retort, "Good night Giovanni." Giovanni never woke again.

During his sleep that night, he dreamed that Katrina was running toward him; her hand reaching out for him. He was smiling as he felt the small, dark-skinned hand take his and literally lift him up. He traveled through space, time and eternity, behind golden wings.

The light was blinding yet it was like he could not see. Then, he felt Ms. Orsini say, "She was quite taken with you." Even though it was something he felt, we will say that Giovanni saw a bright light in the form of a woman holding Katrina's hand. Katrina said, "I am sorry for every time I was frustrating." Giovanni tried to speak but could not. He wanted to say, "I am sorry for every time I was frustrated." It was as if she had shushed him and said, "I know." Then, a great golden-winged, white Angel lifted Giovanni. He could feel the rise of his vibration. It appeared that the metaphorical room became brighter than one could stand. Even the golden-winged, white Angel gazed down. He felt his vibration raise even higher. Then, Giovanni heard but actually felt, "Dear David, I have missed you." Three days had passed.

He found himself with twelve beings of light, all smiling. He was standing, suddenly in a garden, burning on fire. David saw Ariela dive in front of him. A spear had pierced her chest. His blood was boiling as he ran toward the man who had thrown the spear and then suddenly stopped. He turned and ran back to Ariela. He cradled her in his arms as she whispered, "Ahav and Ahava."

David packed up his entire family and moved far away from their home. His struggle was to forgive. He feared he would not control his anger and knew Ariela would want the family to be safe. He also knew with certainty that if he remained, he would retaliate against Ariela's killer.

Then, David saw his life as Henry, a king, ordering boys to war and never quite forgiving himself. It was the love of only one woman, Sussan, which kept him sane. He saw how, as Henry, he had been selfish and withdrew within himself, abandoning his country. His only connection to reality was the voice in his head. Henry's next birth was then planned as an **Aquarian** and with a yellow Angel for selfishness. He also accepted the suggestion as a **Caregiver** *Archetype*. This would ensure he took care of Katrina and himself. Then he saw himself as Giovanni once more, yelling over a teacup. It was not his anger over Katrina's response to the broken teacup but rather the statement that followed: "I can work more hours to buy another teacup but you'll miss me when I'm gone." This was a selfish response by an **Aquarian** who was given a special Angel to help him conquer selfishness. His next life as Robert was planned. He would return under the *Sign* of **Pisces**. Selfishness would follow him. However, he would be given again, a yellow Angel to help him become selfless. David returned to his Pod where he was to ponder his past lives and lessons, preparing for his reincarnation. All the while, David felt Ariela's energy in the adjacent Pod.

*To be continued ...*

## Chapter 14

# Planes ... The Level
# of Vibration

Earth, known as the 1st Plane, is most easily delineated as the physical plane. To describe it, think of water. When water has the lowest energy, it has the lowest vibration. And, in that state, water is a solid.

Now consider Plane 2. This is the transitional or fluid state. This state flows. Consider the involution of the dodecahedron turning in upon itself. To best describe it, picture it as a semisolid form. The soul can literally be poured. To be maintained in a shape, it requires a container. That could be either the dodecahedron or the body. In this state, the soul can literally be felt. This is why, at the level of Plane 2, if you connect to a passed-over soul/waiting to reincarnate, those who are highly sensitive may literally feel them or feel the coolness of their presence. Thus, we can literally just barely pass our hand through water and still feel the coolness of the water.

So, a soul released from Plane 2 flows until it finds the next container which is the body, or in other words ... reincarnation.

Ponder this. The Pod is literally the spiritual womb; flowing to the actual womb; flowing to the actual birth.

The vibration in Plane 2 is just higher than the vibration on Plane 1, the Earth.

The next Plane and higher vibration happens on 3. Consider this the plane of vapor. This is also the plane of Atonement or *life review*. It has a higher vibration than Plane 2. The soul, during its lowest vibration on this plane, may condense and start to flow until it reaches a container. This is the flow from Plane 3 back to Plane 2.

As vibration on this 3rd plane increases, the soul or water dissipates and it is no longer recognizable; it no longer has form. The soul can no longer be contained. It no longer exists as unique except by its common history. In this state, it is only recognizable by its specific vibration or energy. The soul then moves to Plane 4.

Plane 4 is yet higher energy. Regard the vapor as still a form of water. And, as a form of water, if its vibration is lowered, it can return to a lower plane. Thus, souls on this plane, can still return to Earth/reincarnate.

However, if the vibration is raised at this level, it is no longer vapor or water. In this state, there are no longer ties to the physical. But the soul still maintains its common history or memory which is its identity. This is now Plane 5. These souls cannot and do not return to Plane 2 or Plane 1, the Earth. We share our own memories on this level as a means of raising our individual and group vibrations. The more souls on this plane, the higher the vibration.

Plane 6. This is the highest plane created by God. The vibration of two souls is joined. There is synergy which creates more energy than either soul alone. This energy is expansive and cannot be contained by the veil between Plane 1 and Plane 2. Joined souls on Plane 6 actually raise the vibration of all souls, on all planes.

The 7th Plane belongs to God alone until Planes, 1,2,3 and 4 no longer need to exist. Then all planes will have returned home to Plane 7.

This is our Cosmos. There is nothing below Earth and nothing above God. If we examine this more closely, as in the illustration that follows, it should not surprise us that it appears to be resembling Chakras. And, what are Chakras? Man's attempt to describe what affects our Universe or Cosmos from our own ego. Mankind is under the impression that they ARE the Universe and that they created it.

However, we must think about this and explain it from God's perspective since God's is the only one that matters. This is dictated directly to us from our Spirit Guides, the hands of God.

Let's begin with the Root Chakra at the base of the spine. It symbolizes the Earth, Plane 1, and could be the most sluggish area. It is definitely the area that must be cleansed. With the correct balance, there is stability, vibrant energy and growth.

Next, we travel up the body to the Sacral Chakra, located at the lower abdomen or reproductive area. This is the area of birth and death. The correct balance of this Chakra brings happiness, joy, sensuality and creativity. This area should be celebrated! This is the beginning of life; this is the end of life. The illustration coming up shows Plane 2/3, where our Pods are located, and where the tunnel of light is, as well. This is also where Atonement occurs. It is represented by two very important aspects of God; the creative, loving channel and the forgiving channel. For this is where God created you from and this is where God receives you back. God celebrates this with every birth and death. Why would we not celebrate our own sensuality?

Our Solar Plexus is the next area moving up the body. It is located at the navel area, and with balance, there is strength, courage, will power and self-esteem. On our diagram, this would be

Plane 4. This is a plane of strength. It includes our Spirit Guides, Angels and souls with the fortitude to return selflessly to help others. This area also corresponds to our gut! It's the little voice in our head that tells us what is right.

The Heart Chakra comes next, located where we think it should be ... our heart. When this chakra is in balance, we easily give and receive love, acceptance and peace. It also corresponds directly to Plane 5/6. Planes 5 and 6 include those souls who have released the ego and no longer exist making choices based on conceit, selfishness, jealousy and unforgiveness. Their only choice is love.

The Throat Chakra is about communication. It is not located in our throat. But, it extends from the eye of God to Earth, for communication from God extends throughout every plane.

The last two Chakras cannot exist without each other. The Third Eye and the Crown Chakra are located between our two eyes and on the top of our head. These correspond to the 7th Plane. With perfect balance the Third Eye has intuition and creativity. The Crown Chakra in perfect balance has peace and wisdom. Consider the eye of God full of intuition, creativity and the perfect balance of peace and wisdom.

Next is a diagram which represents God's Cosmos or Universe. This is our Universe! It is also the Universe that was created for us not by us. We may believe, if we choose, that there is a Universe that we create ourselves. But that Universe ... would be the one created by our egos. There is no way for our own created Universe to ever be in balance. Because in the Universes created by man, it is believed by them that they get more than they are willing to give and because some of mankind believes the Universe serves them and not others.

God's Universe was created out of love for us not because of us. We cannot command it. Nor does it command us. It accepts us.

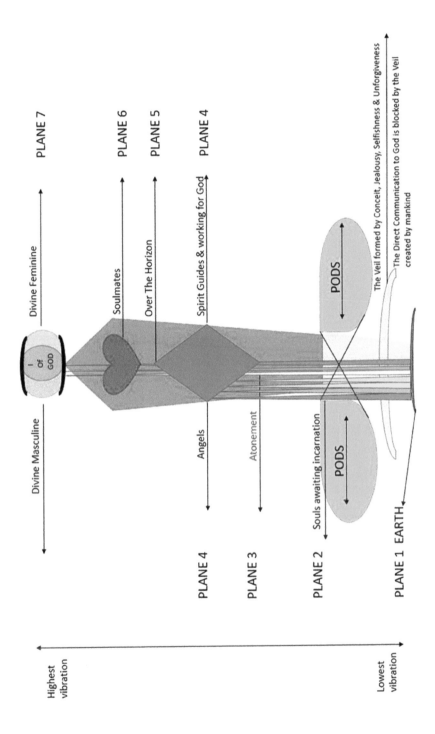

### Plane 1

Earth is the planet on which we live; it is the physical world and all that surrounds it. This includes our sun, moon, our galaxy and all galaxies. It is that which we can experience by our physical senses. It is where mankind defines mankind. It is also how mankind relates to itself by what it can observe in nature.

Man has described what he observes related to the stars. We call these our *Astrological signs*. He observes what he sees in nature; we call these our *Traits*. He observes what he sees in himself and we refer to these as our *Archetypes*. Man has even observed that he has strengths and weaknesses that are of the most basis *Elemental* qualities.

These *Elemental* qualities are so basic to nature, however, there is an undefined nature that helps us learn and grow. We recognize that this force it outside of ourselves. When will we recognize that the forces outside of us are God? For this is the task of Plane 1.

### Plane 2/3

These are the spiritual planes intimately tied to the physical plane of Earth. It is here where we learn that we have a destiny greater than the destiny we create for ourselves on the first plane. We are responsible for our choices. If we accept the responsibility for our choices, we can grow. If we accept our own imperfections, the greatest lesson of karma occurs and we are accepted back home to God.

### Planes 1,2,3,4

We are given the opportunity to reach the potential for which we were created. While on Plane 4, Angels and Spirit Guides reach their potential as they bring us home. Souls may learn their final lessons and return home. Some souls may reach their highest potential and choose to return to assist others. They choose to assist others, even knowing the journey may be difficult.

## Planes 4,5,6

The entities or souls on these planes now serve God. They cannot fathom it any other way. They also now realize that just as they were created in whole, they must return to God in whole. Because, all souls are special just none more special.

Jesus is a brother to all of us. He is a pure soul and part of God's creation. Like all of us, created perfect with free will. Without free will, we cannot love. Because, without given freely, it is not love. And, Jesus gives and gave love freely. So, he returned to God in a near perfect form.

Many have now returned to the spiritual world in this near perfect form. Some have returned this way but were chosen by God, if they so decided to accept the role to remain on a plane close to God, still bathed in God's love and willing to sacrifice, and yet return to the Earth upon God's request. Again, as we said before, these souls may be asked to return to Earth to help others.

Others on this plane (4 on the diagram) have reached a level not quite perfect and are still working toward their path of completion. God offers them a position or assignment to help them toward perfection. These souls realize that they may be asked to return to Earth for several reasons eventually, should they not succeed in their position. Or, if they do succeed, they may either pass onto a plane (5 and above on diagram) and never need to return to Earth or remain on Plane 4 to accept a request specifically by God to return to Earth for a purpose.

Just as Angels and Spirit Guides these souls that experience level four serve as a connection directly from God to the Earth. They serve as lesser vibrational beings than the full vibrational being which is God.

Angels and our main Spirit Guides cannot come to Earth as humans. However, these lesser vibrational souls can. And, these 4th-Plane souls are on a much higher vibration than those souls awaiting to return on Plane 2.

Those on Plane 4 have no hierarchy. No one is more advanced than another as they are all on the same vibrational level. There are no Archangels, just Angels. There are no superior Spirit Guides, just Spirit Guides. God does not consider the 4th Plane souls any less than the souls on Plane 5. However, God does see specific strengths and abilities that make it possible for these souls to return to Earth, carry out a purpose, engage in karma and still find their way back to God. And, that may take more than one life. Often, the lessons are what these souls are capable of handling.

## Plane 5

We refer to going to the 5th plane as being Over the Horizon.

Metaphorically, this means that over the horizon is a new day. The physical first plane will never be experienced again. We will never again experience the separation from God. Our focus then is only on others. We experience joy in the return of every soul. We also experience God's joy with each and every returned soul. It is this joy that it now our joy. And, it is this love that is now our love.

## Plane 6

Plane 6 is a unique and beautiful plane. It is a plane that celebrates **LOVE.** Two individual souls who have experienced many lives together and have grown both individually as well as together, representing a completeness of all masculine and feminine qualities related to love, may be asked individually by God upon completion of their return, to join as a new creation.

This creation is called *soulmates.* A masculine and a feminine soul is not the requirement rather, the exemplification of the love the two souls displayed. Love is love. And, a soul may be any sex.

### Plane 7

God is alone, awaiting the return of all souls to return home. God is complete in all masculine and feminine qualities. And, all of those qualities see … through one eye.

God gave us creation out of love and out of acceptance which is also love, God welcomes us home. Thus, God created us all at once, and will accept all of us back to Plane 7, together.

In conclusion, when the last soul has completed their path and has reached Plane 5, all souls will be accepted into Plane 7 by God.

# Part IV

## GOD

## Chapter 15
# Joyful Hallelujah,
# My Child Has Returned

*Dave ...*

These are the words spoken to ME, directly from God. It was as if there were two speaking at once. It was like the two were having a conversation with one another and with me.

In an attempt to explain this experience, I would say that during one moment there was roaring power. The next moment it was soft. It was as if a gong and a tiny little bell were enacting together. The words were placed tenderly into my thoughts.

It felt as if the incarnation to Earth was pertinent to knowing the difference in roughness and free will, versus the absolute pull of love and softness from God. I felt that the separation from all others that are not God is as painful to God as it is the others away from God.

On the rose every petal is exactly perfect. That is how I felt God viewed all of the others who are not God.

Rain and sunshine are love from God. Every lesson is a nourishment to help us. The conflicts are within all others; not within God.

The release of the ego is more joyous than I can explain. I felt it explode within God's words. That is love.

*God Speaks ...*

*I AM I AM. I AM one. One is love. Two is love. Others are not one. Others are ordered, numbered, named, listed.*

*No flower is exactly the same. Flowers bloom when they are nourished. I AM love, and love nourishes. All are from one.*

*Light is from one. Light nourishes. Why would the sun shine without love? Others would not shine or survive in separation if not created as others.*

*Free will and manifestation of destiny is like a blooming of the flower. Only in this earthly existence is the light sustaining. I AM justification and creation. I AM beauty, light and love. Others must be with others.*

*It makes what seems imprisonment of separation bearable. Two others with free will, will have conflict based on ego. Conflict based on ego is conceit, jealousy, selfishness and unforgiveness.*

*Each rose as unique as the next, each ruby as unique as the next. The roses flourish and are beautiful even with the thorns. Two roses that flourish together are unaware of their thorns.*

*Two roses can become a bush which literally becomes a tree. Even as the petals fall, the bush remains strong. It grows, it evolves and it creates more flowers.*

*When the bush becomes aware the creation of the flower is more important than the creation of the thorn, the bush reaches its potential. Other needs other, to learn, grow and evolve.*

*When ego lets go, others bloom.*

*I have numbered, named, listed, not forgotten. I have nurtured. I have watered and I AM love.*

*When ego forgives conflict, love prevails. Love prevails, love returns, others are one, others are love, I AM one. Joyful Hallelujah. My child, my other, has returned. I AM one.*

# Part V

## Elizabeth

## Chapter 16

## Love

*Elizabeth speaks ...*

God is love. We are created in God's image; we are created as love.

From the beginning, we have been the elected, the chosen. There are none that are nonchosen.

Is it the tree of life or is it a rose bush? Is this Moses's burning bush?

All are special, none are more special. You cannot be owned thus you must have free will. The rose must be nurtured even if it has thorns. Self-respect is about being your best self. You must know yourself, with humility.

Love is patient, love is kind, love is disappointed but not angry. Love seeks truth, truth seeks love. Respect the love, with humility.

There is responsibility for freedom. Each rose petal is attached to the rose. Each rose is attached to the stem. Each stem is attached to the root. However, each plant is from one seed.

If one rose falls, we do not dig up the plant. In fact, when that rose falls, it just forms another root.

It works the same with the daisy. For the rose accepts the daisy as part of the garden. For the rose and the daisy are both of the same creation.

There is great wisdom in nature. Wisdom is love. Nature nourishes the rose. Nature provides sunshine and rain. It provides sunshine and gentle rain and the rose grows. Nature does not tell the rose to grow. Sometimes nature seems harsh. But even the rose will grow after a flood. A rose never asks the question: "Why am I a rose?" The rose confidently says, "I was created to bloom."

Fear not nature. Nature is meant to cleanse and nourish. Nature may ignite a fire in you. Nature may breathe life into you. Nature nourishes you with water and provides earth for you to be rooted. If you only see nature as the storm, you will not see the beauty in a peaceful, tranquil body of water. Does not the storm provide for the water?

Humans have been created with infinite potential and that potential is love. With that potential comes responsibility. Human minds are so powerful that they can make choices on Earth that will affect their destiny. However, humans do not have the power to choose away their responsibility. The human mind may attempt to create many realities and if this comforts you, so be it. You cannot escape your responsibilities.

What is the past but lessons? What is nature but lessons? Examine both and the lessons equal compassion.

God is love. You are created in the image of love.

Ahav and Ahava.

*Love, Elizabeth ...*

**Please, thank you and you're welcome!**

*The life after Katrina and Giovanni's ...*

A child was born, then another child.

*I* created these two souls with the infinite potential to love. A **Warm** *Traited* **Aquarian** and a **Warm** *Traited* **Pisces,** they were. Both accepted the **Lover** *Archetype.* There was always meant to be a connection. She the **Aquarian** would add strength to him the **Pisces.** His soft nature as a **Pisces** would be her love.

Her *Archetype* was modified with two **Fires.** His *Archetype* was modified with **Fire** and **Water.** Love would blossom but not burn out.

Sarah would not own Robert and Robert would not own Sarah. Neither one more special than the other, but both special. Each complementing the other.

There was no obstacle they could not overcome with love, including her death. Sarah and Robert continued to give, even in her death.

Ahav and Ahava (*Love and love given without expectation*).

Joyful Hallelujah!

This was truly a blossoming rose in the *IMAGE* of love.

*I AM LOVE*

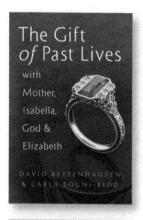

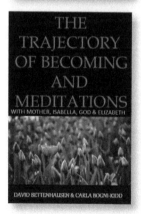

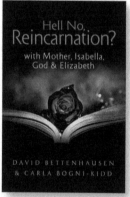

Coming soon

Dave and Carla share their experiences with the world through meditation and their writing.

Following the path of love and forgiveness rather than one with conceit, jealousy and selfishness is the message. We can overcome our karma when following these five simple rules.

*The Manual* is the third of their released books and *The Trajectory of Becoming and Meditations* is coming soon.

Visit: thegiftofpastlives .com for more information.

Lightning Source UK Ltd.
Milton Keynes UK
UKHW022220070122
396800UK00006B/78